The Career Survival Guide

Brian O'Connell

McGraw-Hill

New York   Chicago   San Francisco   Lisbon   London
Madrid   Mexico City   Milan   New Delhi
San Juan   Seoul   Singapore   Sydney   Toronto

The **McGraw·Hill** Companies

1 2 3 4 5 6 7 8 9 0   AGM/AGM   0 9 8 7 6 5 4 3

ISBN 0-07-139130-4

McGraw-Hill books are available at special quantity discounts to use as premiums and sales promotions, or for use in corporate training programs. For more information, please write to the Director of Special Sales, Professional Publishing, McGraw-Hill, Two Penn Plaza, New York, NY 10121-2298. Or contact your local bookstore.

This book is printed on recycled, acid-free paper containing a minimum of 50% recycled, de-inked fiber.

Library of Congress Cataloging-in-Publication Data

O'Connell, Brian, 1959-
The career survival guide / Brian O'Connell.
     p.   cm.
  Includes index.
  ISBN 0-07-139130-4 (alk. paper)
  1. Career development.   2. Success in business.   I. Title.

HF5381.O34   2002
650.14—dc21   2002023139

Contents

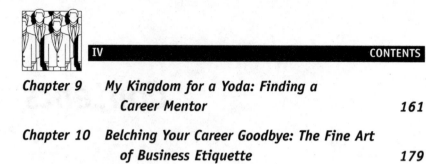

Preface

There's an old line about finding a job you love and adding five days to your week. Beyond the fact that I wish I'd said it first, this adage pretty much sums up what this book is all about—finding the job you want and building on it not only to survive in the corporate jungle but also to thrive in it. These days, this is not easy.

The last few years have been tough for working professionals. Over two million jobs were lost in the United States during 2000 and 2001. The first wave of dot-coms turned out to be "dot-bombs," and New Economy professionals found that Old Economy companies weren't hiring. Professionals found that when you combine the New Economy with the Old Economy, you got "No Economy" (in the short term anyway). It was the rare employee who didn't have his blood flowing backward through his veins as he made that long walk to the human resources department, pink slip in hand, on the way to a spirit-crushing exit interview.

Seasoned careerists have seen tough times before. In fact, recessions—and the waves of pink slips that go with them—have kicked off our last four decades dating back to the 1970s. Many people know what it takes to stay afloat during stormy economies, if not create opportunities to get ahead in them. But the new wave of 20- and 30-somethings in the twenty-first-century workplace never really knew a tough job climate until the Internet boom caved in. Suddenly they went from calling the shots to downing them at their favorite watering holes, unable to regain the hefty salaries, high titles, and social cachet they enjoyed as founding members of the dot-com generation.

Whether you're an ex-dot-commer pining for the stock option salad days or a 40-something professional reaching for that next rung on the career ladder, the keys to getting ahead in the workplace are the same in good times and in bad. When managers look for candidates to promote in good times or to hang onto during a layoff, they look for the same qualities and characteristics. At the same time, they're looking for characteristics—or red flags—that they don't want in an employee.

The aim of this book is not only to introduce you to the character traits and individual qualities that companies look for in employees and the ones they don't but also to demonstrate how to emphasize those positive qualities while negating the negative ones. There is no payoff for being lazy on the job, for being surly, or for being a political backstabber.

But there is a payoff for shaking off any anxieties and insecurities left over from both the dot-com demise and the terrorist attacks on New York City and Washington that combined not only to cripple our economy and job market but also to leave us questioning our career choices. Facing layoffs at work and uncertainty at home, Americans have become stronger and more resilient in the face of adversity, much like many of our parents and grandparents did in World Wars I and II.

Reinvigorated, we returned to the workplace determined to make more of our lives both at home and at work. While I don't pretend to be much help on the home front (I have enough trouble keeping my three kids in line), I am confident that I can help you to get your career on track, to become a more valuable commodity in the workplace, and to win the recognition, both financial and professional, that you deserve.

Not only could this add five days to your week, but it also could add many happy years to your life.

Brian O'Connell
Doylestown, Pennsylvania
November 2002

1

New Economy or Old Economy, the Times They Are a Changin'

As career professionals we've never really come to grips with adversity.

Sure, we toe the party line and tell ourselves the latest spittle-laced fusillade from the boss or the recent 10-round bout with the office psychopath is "character building." But that doesn't mean we like it any better.

Still, there is a lot to say in defense of the "adversity" thing. The famous writer Pearl S. Buck once said of adversity, "We learn as much from sorrow as from joy, as much from illness as from health, from handicap as from advantage—and indeed perhaps more."

Consider the real-world example of Edmund McIlhenny. A sugar magnate in Civil War–era Louisiana, McIlhenny had to flee in advance of the Union Army's arrival in 1863. Upon his return two

1

years later, he found his sugar plantation decimated and unusable for that agricultural purpose. Undaunted—and more than a bit hungry—McIlhenny picked some hot Mexican peppers whose seeds had fallen to the soil months earlier. Encouraged by their spiciness, he started fooling around with different recipes before finally settling on the one we know today as Tabasco sauce. His resiliency and ability to adjust to the situation around him made him a much wealthier Tabasco titan than he was a sugar magnate.

Like McIlhenny, the great American white-collar worker has experienced adversity in recent years.

American career professionals certainly have felt their share of adversity in recent years. After a 10-year run from 1990 to 2000 that was the envy of the global markets, the U.S economy crash-landed shortly after the birth of the twenty-first century. Many overvalued Internet companies imploded, leaving behind a wide swath of laid-off workers clutching pink slips in one hand and worthless stock options in the other.

On September 11, 2001, things got worse in a hurry. The terrorist attacks on New York City and Washington not only rendered Americans numb emotionally but also left the rest of the economy—what pundits like to call the Old Economy—in tatters as well. Factory orders declined, consumer spending spiked downward, the housing market dropped precipitously, and millions more workers lost their jobs.

The timing for the American workforce could not have been worse. Economic conditions deteriorated just as the American workplace was figuring out how to blend New Economy innovation into Old Economy bottom-line values. Sure, information technology had changed enough that a musical microchip pasted on a greeting card now packs more computing power than could be found in any computer in the world in 1950. But did enough people want to buy musical greeting cards to build a new industry around them? The answer was no.

This is just for starters—other economic factors began to have an impact on American working professionals as well.

THE GLOBAL ECONOMY

All of a sudden it was not unusual for a U.S. clothing company to design a suit in Korea, buy fabric in Australia, have the suit sewn in Taiwan, hold the suit in a warehouse in Puerto Rico, and sell it in Europe. Such globe-trotting strategies called for new skills and responsibilities from employees. Being passed over because you didn't speak Spanish was no longer considered a shock around water coolers and watering holes.

Employees who best accommodated such changes in U.S. business practices were the ones who knew how to adapt. For example, workers who blended easily into team atmospheres and who could respond efficiently to change found themselves in demand. So too did employees who knew how to place a high priority on customer service and satisfaction and who did so in different languages and time zones.

THE NEW ECONOMY (AND ITS RELATIONSHIP WITH THE OLD ECONOMY)

There's no question that a huge factor in the workplace dynamic these days is the New Economy, which almost became the "No Economy" before being merged with the Old Economy (got that?).

Before I talk about the impact of the New Economy (and the Old Economy) on the way we look at our careers, let me first provide some background. The Old Economy is personified by such companies as Ford Motor Company and Procter & Gamble, which comprise the Dow Jones Industrial Average. The New Economy is comprised of NASDAQ newcomers such as eBay, Amazon.com, and Oracle.

To corporations and entrepreneurs (the people who hire us), the New Economy means new markets and new opportunities to consider (such as biotechnology and the Internet), new channels for transacting, and a plethora of new investment opportunities to explore (such as wireless telecom and real-time Web technologies). The Old Economy? It's Fritos and fan belts, bedspreads and broomsticks. You know—products that people actually use.

Most business observers define the New Economy as a global economy where information is as much a commodity as beer or Barbie dolls. It's an economy in which communications technology creates geographically borderless competition—not just for brews and Barbies but also for mortgage loans and other services that aren't packed into a box and sent rolling down loading docks.

This is just the nuts and bolts, however. Before the dot-com implosion of 2000 and 2001, the New Economy also had a new frontier, wild, wild West ring about it that American baby boomers weaned on John Wayne and Clint Eastwood seemed to love. In the New Economy, chaos was considered creative. Horizons were short. Employees paid no deference to their elders. The young tried to eat the old. Every successful company in Silicon Valley seemed to beget a more successful one that made employees, if not smug, at least immune to the notion that things could go sour and that pink slips would soon rain down from the sky on millions of workers who considered themselves bulletproof.

When it became apparent to the professional investors on Wall Street that the value of New Economy companies was vastly inflated, they picked up their marbles and went home. This resulted in a catastrophic domino effect, as suddenly cash-strapped entrepreneurs got on their cell phones and speed-dialed their investors looking for more infusions of cash. Like a chronic gambler who keeps going back to the betting window for another shot, however, the entrepreneurs found that venture capitalists had stopped returning their phone calls.

Short on money and time, many dot-com business owners pulled the plug, sending millions of shocked employees out into the streets, clutching their "Leftovers.com" coffee mug in one hand and a fistful of worthless stock options in the other.

At about the same time, the Old Economy companies, many of which had made massive investments in New Economy companies, decided to take some, but not all, of the dot-com workforce into their happy fold. Such companies as Barnes and Noble and Citibank, which had figured out how to merge their bricks-and-mortar business components with their Internet businesses, welcomed the technological know-how that the ex–New Economy workers they hired brought to the table. Other Old Economy companies followed suit, but not nearly enough to hire the army of software engineers, Web content managers, graphic designers, and account managers wandering the streets looking for work.

Even though many dot-coms crashed, the New Economy, personified by the Internet, remains the single most important factor in commerce, communications, education, medicine, and every other field that requires human interaction. Obviously, it is *not* going away, and it will rise once again in stature, although it may not get within shouting distance of its heights in the late 1990s. Still, the roller-coaster ride on which the New Economy took legions of workers has left a bitter taste that won't easily go away. The idea that the Internet empowered employees and gave them more leverage in the workplace than ever before was a tempting one. After all, how can you argue with six-figure salaries, comfy telecommuting gigs, and ballooning stock option programs? This is why when the bubble finally burst it seemed like a death in the family. First, there was shock, then denial, then frustration, and then, as always, the insecurity that inevitably follows a deep, negative life experience.

It was a wake-up call that we're still waking up to, but the lessons learned from our workplace experiences in the New Economy bring into focus many of the career-advancement values and strategies that you'll find in this book.

INFORMATION TECHNOLOGY

New workplace initiatives such as flextime, independent contractors, and telecommuting could never exist without the toys and tools that high technology has developed. Few would argue that the Internet, fax machines, cellular telephones, and other related technologies make it possible for workers to work away from the office on a full-time basis. This concept is revolutionizing the typical day at the office.

It's no secret that computer knowledge will be essential for your work life. Let's face it, traditional work as we know it is disappearing. High-tech gadgets now operate machinery for banking, parts assembly, warehouse inventory, truck and taxi dispatching, and driver's license renewals. Brand-new jobs are constantly being created to develop and run computer hardware, software, and networks. This means that forward-thinking professionals will have to upgrade their work-related skills continually to keep pace with rapid changes in technology.

But information technology is affecting American working professionals in ways that high-tech tool developers likely didn't imagine—or at least didn't let on about if they did imagine them. Sure, information technology made us better workplace "producers," but this has meant bringing the workplace with us wherever we go, via laptop computers, personal digital assistants, cell phones, and fax machines.

Such high-tech instruments were supposed to free us from the surly bonds of inefficiency. But in a pact with the devil that would make Machiavelli proud, we've traded higher productivity for a good chunk of our personal freedom. Think about it. Did you check your e-mail on your last vacation? Do you bring your cell phone to dinners? Ballgames? Your daughter's ballet recital (hopefully not)?

Our dependence on our telecommunications toys reveals an insecurity toward our jobs and careers that we don't want to think about. A secure vice president at a large bank might not dash off and take a phone call at her son's birthday party at Chucky Cheese. If she did, however, she'd easily rationalize it by elevating the importance of the call to the military equivalent of DefCon 5. Two forces are gnawing away at executives in moments such as those: the responsibility of family (it doesn't have to be a mother at a birthday party; it could just as easily be a singleton at his parents' house for Thanksgiving dinner or an empty-nester out with friends on bowling night) and the responsibility toward one's career. Our kids, our families, and our friends aren't going to fire us. They might roll their eyes, but they understand our commitment to our careers.

But your boss on the other end of the line—who doesn't care if he is interrupting your personal life—*can* fire you if you don't take the call—or at least question your dedication to the firm and use his influence to derail you from your firm's fast track.

Twenty-five years ago, the notion of being wired into your workplace from your home, your car, or a jet airliner 30,000 feet above

Phoenix was a fantasy. Sure, your dad might have brought home a briefcase crammed with paperwork once in a while, but it was the exception rather than the rule. The advent of the New Economy, which among other delights promised to abolish the paper-strewn office and replace it with a digital one we could carry around with us, stirred something deep inside us career-wise.

Here was a chance to become more productive—to show our employers what we could really do if given the right tools. I remember the crushing disappointment at one of my first jobs on a Wall Street bond desk when I was deemed unworthy of receiving a corporate cell phone. The fact that I was a trading assistant who merely executed trades, worked the phones, and compiled everything into a neat little package at the end of the trading day had nothing to do with it. So what if the market closed at 4:00? So what if my bosses, portfolio managers, and senior managers mostly, never needed to reach me when the markets were closed? So what if I rarely traveled or took part in social events away from the office during trading hours? I wanted that $#@&! phone. I raged silently as my workplace "superiors" grabbed those gleaming new cell phones with the zeal of Anna Nicole Smith glomming phone numbers at a Metamucil convention.

Alas I didn't get one, and sure enough, creeping insecurity shortly turned into raging paranoia when management began giving laptops away to "critical" workers a few months later. I felt like one of those "unnecessary" government workers who gets to go home in snowstorms and other natural disasters. Unnecessary? Me? Somebody pass me the Valium.

As I progressed in my career, I began noticing that these mobile office products were as much a curse as they were a blessing. Sure, getting a company-paid cell phone seems like a badge of honor. Sooner or later, however, the lucky recipient finds himself tethered to the workplace, always a phone call away from the boss or the big client.

THE INTERNET

Despite the dot-com disasters of 2000 and 2001, there's no doubt that the broader perspective that the Web has given global businesses has taken hold in boardrooms like barnacles to the side of a boat. Indeed, the Web has helped businesses of all sizes find opportunities in the international marketplace; know more about their competition in the United States and around the world; advertise and sell their products to global audiences through their Web sites; use e-mail as a way to communicate with employees, suppliers, and buyers; and use business-to-business (B2B) connections to help their businesses grow.

For career professionals, the Internet meant having to handle increasing amounts of information, develop excellent communication skills, and upgrade their technology skills continuously.

The Internet has had a special impact on small businesses in that computerization and use of the Internet have allowed them to level the playing field in global commerce. The Internet also allows small companies to advertise equally with big companies and target customers in specialized markets—markets too small for big businesses that have to sell to millions of people to be profitable.

THE CHANGING WORKPLACE

The way Americans view the workplace and their careers has changed as well. Instead of landing a nice, steady job for 30 years like their dads (and some moms) did, American workers count on landing five or six steady jobs in their lifetimes, bracing themselves for a constant retooling of skills in the process.

The workplace changed along with workers' attitudes toward their careers as new technology breakthroughs such as e-mail and voice mail stripped the traditional workplace of its boundaries, making any car, living room, airplane, or commuter train a branch office. Toss into the mix corporate downsizing and outsourcing, global competition, two-earner families, independent contracting, wage stagnation, workplace anxiety, office politics, and surly bosses, and it's no wonder that so many working professionals felt stifled, confused, and even fearful about their careers.

The good news is that, by and large, U.S. businesses of all sizes are trying to keep workers—those who haven't been pink-slipped anyway—satisfied and productive. More and more companies have adopted policies that accommodate workers' busy lives. Flexible work arrangements, telecommuting, performance-based compensation programs, profit-sharing plans, and fatter benefits packages have become standard operating procedure for companies that want to attract the best talent possible.

INDEPENDENT CONTRACTORS

Raise a glass to the fearless freelancer, willing to forgo such trivial tokens as a regular paycheck and company-paid benefits to be the boss.

The Internet has had much to do with the upward trend in free-lancing as well. Because of trends such as globalization, companies can't afford to have full-time employees available on a 24/7/365 basis. Consequently, businesses have stepped up the rate at which they hire part-time workers, launch job-sharing programs, or contract work out to freelancers.

While doing without a regular paycheck and having to pay for their own health benefits in the bargain, millions of Americans have turned to independent contracting, rolling out new desktop publishing, Web content-producing, or public relations businesses and have found themselves in demand and in the driver's seat of their own careers.

BUILDING YOUR OWN BRAND

Remember that old Chinese proverb, "May you live in interesting times"? History will no doubt record the turn of the twenty-first century as one for the books. The advancement of the Internet, the rise of global terrorism, and the shift to global markets will fill chapters of their own in future academic tomes.

Perhaps a separate chapter will be written in history books about the metamorphosis of the modern worker from a corporate lifer to an independent-minded master of her own career.

I call such workers *gold-collar workers*—the people who take more responsibility for their careers, constantly assess their strengths and weaknesses, and plan career paths like a military commander draws up a battlefield plan. Today's gold-collar professionals understand that the days when anyone could step into a lifetime job with regular pay raises, promotions, and a good pension at retirement are a thing of the past, gone the way of the slide rule, the drive-in movie, and the Hula Hoop.

Recognizing that workers without something to offer will face significant career difficulties, gold-collar workers will upgrade their skills and retrain themselves constantly. They will learn to understand the entire business, not just their own jobs. They will learn marketable skills they can take from company to company. They will understand that in a tough job climate, companies will cling to their best employees instead of vice versa. They will be curious, constantly researching their fields of career interest and keeping an eye on trends to anticipate what will happen in their industries.

Gold-collar workers also will be opportunity makers, looking for areas that lack skilled workers and building their knowledge in those areas. They will create networks, recognizing that their contacts may be lifelines to the work they want to get.

In short, gold-collar workers will be in demand.

And this book will show you how to become one.

Workplace Trends in the Early 2000s

- In 1994, 62 percent of the jobs that were eliminated were supervisory, managerial, or professional (compared with 44 percent in 1991), and 85 percent of those who have lost white-collar jobs will never get them back.
- Work that used to require 100 workers a few years ago can be done by 50 today and probably 10 tomorrow.
- Jobs are a social artifact—intelligence is the new form of property.
- We work, on average, 20 hours more per month than our parents did after World War II.
- Eighty percent of jobs will be taken over by automation or cheaper labor in other countries.
- Thirty-five percent of North Americans in the labor force either are unemployed or are temporary, part-time, or contractual workers (in Europe, the figure is 50 percent).
- The employee-employer contract has now been broken, and loyalty to the organization no longer ensures job security.
- Technology is complex, and no one person can "know" a function completely; thus we will need to collaborate with each other.

Continued

- Organizations are becoming flatter and more horizontal.
- Bureaucracy is ineffective when dealing with the multidimensional complexity caused by the diversity of customers, employees, partners, suppliers, and technologies.
- Function-based work involving single-skilled workers is being replaced by project-based work involving multiskilled knowledge workers.
- Loyalty to traditional businesses will make a comeback. With the dot-com frenzy subsiding and career opportunities in that sector becoming less attractive, many workers will return to traditional corporate jobs with a renewed appreciation for their stability and structure.
- Corporate culture will be critical for attracting new talent. Individuals will seek employers who are committed to fostering a dynamic and challenging work environment, one in which opportunities to hone new skills abound and in which flexible work schedules and telecommuting are possible.
- Employers will get better at letting people go. Because the manner in which an employer lays off employees has a direct impact on its reputation and ultimately its future recruitment and retention efforts, human resources professionals will be placing further emphasis on establishing sound employee separation practices to manage organizational change and resulting job losses effectively.
- Older workers will get creative in finding new employment. Individuals over age 50 will enjoy greater opportunities to craft unique employment positions for themselves. To combat perceptions that they are less open to new ideas and are a risky investment because they are so close to retirement, they will propose creative contractual and consulting arrangements with potential employers.
- Companies will address the e-communication overload. As a result of e-mail depersonalizing the workplace, more

Continued

employers will take a closer look at how their workforces use e-mail to ensure that the long-standing benefits of traditional communication techniques do not become a thing of the past.

—Used by permission of www.itstime.com

REALITY CHECK: THE KEY TO WORKPLACE SUCCESS? START EARLY

When did Ed O'Neill know he was going to become director of sales at his giant biotechnology firm?

When he was 15 years old.

Even at that age Ed knew he wanted to have a big career in sales. Juggling a paper route and a job as a caddy at the local golf course along with his schoolwork, the affable teenager found he liked dealing with people and getting them to see his side of things. He became an expert at finagling an extra five dollars or so from his golfing clients by going the extra mile wading into ponds to snag errant golf balls or fetching them cold drinks between holes. He liked the give and take of the business world, and he recognized early on that he had a knack for influencing other people's decisions.

Twenty-five years later Ed is still hustling, still making sure that his customers get what they need when they need it. Only now he's calling the shots for a 250-employee department with a $30 million annual budget.

Oh, and he's still not above hiking his pants up and going after a client's wayward tee-shot at corporate gold outings. That will never change.

2

You, Inc.—The Rise of the Gold-Collar Worker

We'll spend a lot of time in this book discussing the key attributes career professionals must display to get ahead in the workplace. One of those attributes, I believe, takes precedence over any other, and that is "attitude." You know, the kind of "can-do" attitude your mom and dad were forever lecturing you about.

Guess what? Mom and Dad had a point.

History is rich with tales of the difference a positive attitude can make. Ben Franklin demonstrated it at the birth of our nation. At a meeting in Parliament in 1774, Franklin watched in dismay as British leaders tore into the ungrateful inhabitants of the New World to the west. Disgusted at their high-handedness, Franklin made up his mind right then and there to no longer consider himself a Briton but an American. In the ensuing years, his valuable business and political acumen—and some nice contacts—helped America finance its successful revolution over King George, culminating in Washington's victory over Cornwallis at Yorktown.

Or how about Abraham Lincoln, who though his heart sank at the thought of the casualties spawned by the Civil War, presided over the war, knowing that the Union had to be saved at any cost? An unwavering commitment to that end made history.

The business world is no different. Just recently, Hewlett-Packard chief executive Carly Fiorina won a hard-fought battle against the relatives of her famous company's founders and seemingly the entire business media—who said that her proposed merger with Compaq would never win shareholder approval. Undaunted, Fiorina plowed ahead, winning the votes she needed to clear the way for an HP/Compaq alliance. A hundred years earlier, Henry Ford showed the same moxie, repeatedly turning a deaf ear to his friend Thomas Edison's admonitions against the viability of a motor car. History showed that even the great Edison was wrong once in a while.

FAILURE IS NOT AN OPTION

Historians might say that what these innovators had in common was the elusive trait of genius. Maybe so. But I prefer to think that they succeeded because of bulldogged determination to prevail, damn the odds. I love the quote from the NASA mission commander played by actor Ed Harris in *Apollo 13*. Faced with a seemingly impossible task of bringing the Apollo 13 astronauts back from space safely, Harris coolly replied, "Failure is not an option."

When it comes to your career, failure should never be an option. W. A. Nance once said that people who fail can be divided into those who thought and never did and those who did and never thought. Certainly, a positive attitude is at the top of the list in shaping what some career experts call *gold-collar workers.* This is a term I love because it accurately identifies the career professional who wants to get ahead in the workplace and knows how to go about it.

What is a gold-collar worker? A worker who combines the attributes of attitude, ambition, enthusiasm, integrity, determination, discipline, and work ethics to become a lean, mean, career-advancing machine. Gold-collar workers can work on a manufacturing plant line, pound out software code in a cubicle, or write advertising copy. They are not easily pigeonholed by age, gender, ethnicity, or any other demographic a pointy-headed academic can roll out. What makes them stand out in a crowd is their record of achievement in their careers and the smiles on their faces due to the fact that they're doing what they love to do.

Chances are we all have the attributes that personify a gold-collar worker. The challenge is demonstrating those attributes and allowing ourselves to shine through the traditional barriers that keep us from reaching our career goals.

"Hey," you might say reading this, "I have all those attributes, but nobody's calling me a gold-collar worker." But success transcends simply having the tools to succeed. Gold-collar workers are career professionals who take these attributes and use them creatively. Here are some examples.

A gold-collar worker is someone who . . .

- *Is enthusiastic.* Enthusiasm, like measles, mumps, and the common cold, is highly contagious. If you could bottle enthusiasm, you'd make billions.
- *Actively seeks to get ahead.* For example, when a gold-collar worker is alone in the office with her supervisor, the gold-collar invariably asks if there's anything she can do to help

the supervisor. In effect, the gold-collar worker is asking, "How can I make a larger contribution?" Contributions are what make successful careers, at least in the long run. Gold-collar workers are never passive. This is why they are promoted and then promoted again.

- *Knows the lay of the land.* Gold-collar workers know how their workplaces operate. They've figured out whether most promotions are based on creativity or detail ability, sales or production/operations experience, computer or interpersonal skills. Then they work on the skills needed to capitalize on their workplace's culture.

- *Creates opportunities—and takes responsibility.* Ideas are the lifeblood of the workplace. Consequently, gold-collar workers constantly deliver well-researched ideas and then volunteer to take charge of their execution. Initiative is another way of saying that you deserve a promotion. Allow me to expand on this trait with some real-world examples. Consider the problem of pesky telemarketers, who can call you at work and disrupt your focus. While pacing the floor waiting for an important call, attorney Ken Jursinski's assistant buzzed to say there was an emergency on the line. It turned out to be some guy trying to sell him stocks. For Ken, the time had come to stop complaining about the problem of unwanted solicitations and to start solving it. Four years later he was selling the Phone Butler, a device he invented to give unwanted callers the polite brush-off. Users press the star button, and a gentle but firm voice with a British accent says, "Pardon me, this is the Phone Butler, and I have been directed to inform you that this household must respectfully decline your inquiry. Kindly place this number on your do-not-call list. Good day." Then there's Ellen Phillips, a middle-school English, drama, and speech teacher who excelled at the rather obscure art of the written consumer complaint. Egged on by coworkers, Phillips built a lucrative sideline exacting justice for other people's complaints. For a fee, Ellen's Poison Pen (www.ellenphillips.net) will write a reasoned letter of complaint and follow up with persistent action. Both Jursinki and Phillips saw an opportunity and ran with it. This is a lesson worth learning.

- *Becomes an expert in a specific field.* Yogi Berra once said that you can learn a lot by watching. True enough. Watch and listen long enough, and you could soon become an expert in your field. Rather than sitting and waiting for someone to come along and proclaim them an expert, as too many workplace denizens do, gold-collar workers go out and become such experts. Whether it's going back to school to learn Excel, offering to write about it for an industry trade magazine, or even offering to talk about it in front of a Chamber of Commerce group, gold-collar workers won't hesitate—and more important, aren't afraid—to become an industry expert. Imagine giving a speech on manufacturing line innovations and noticing that your boss is in the audience. Or maybe even better, your future boss. One more thing. Becoming an expert is hard work. When Thomas Edison was asked to explain his genius, he answered, "It's 99 percent perspiration and 1 percent inspiration."

- *Treats his or her career as a small business.* Gold-collar workers take control of their own careers. They don't like leaving things to chance and possibly seeing someone else take control of their workplace reputations. Like the neighborhood grocer or that software startup out by the interstate, gold-collar workers take their reputations and responsibilities personally. If clients aren't happy, gold-collar workers learn that old small-business trick of "killing them with kindness" and making them happy customers once again. And remember, thinking like a small business owner enables you to react fast to problems.

- *Knows his or her industry cold.* Gold-collar workers can just about cite chapter and verse what their industry is up to on a daily basis. This sounds tough, especially for ultrabusy people like single parents or professionals who volunteer in their community. But all that becoming savvy about your industry entails is reading the industry newsletter or checking out the *Wall Street Journal* or *Business Week* or the industry trade publications that are invariably lying about the workplace. Even better is developing your own contacts in the industry and chatting them up once a week or so. The Web is a big help, too. Industry associations almost always have Web sites chock full of information and data on your business. Or subscribe to an online clipping service that will e-mail you news and information on your business community. Lexus-Nexus (www.lexusnexus.com), and Northern Light (www.northernlight.com) are good places to start. So are Business Wire (www.businesswire.com), Google.com (www.google.com), and PR Newswire (www.prnewswire.com).

- *Knows the value of a mentor.* Gold-collar workers align themselves with people who can champion their progress inside the executive boardroom. In a smaller business, this can be the chief executive officer (CEO) or the office administrator. In larger businesses, a mentor can be the director of one's own department—or another department—or simply a coworker who's got the ear of company decision makers.

- *Develops a fat Rolodex.* Collecting business cards might seem like a waste of time to some people, but gold-collar workers know that a phone number here or an e-mail address there can come in handy down the road. If you're attending a conference and don't have business cards to hand out or don't work hard to hand them out, you might be missing out on a bigger and better opportunity down the road. Contacts also come in handy when you are looking for good information on your industry. While nobody likes a pest, one thing I've learned in the journalism business is that people love to talk if you give them a chance. Part of networking is also realizing what you can do for others. John F. Kennedy may have had patriotism on his mind when he famously spoke, "Ask not what your country can do for you, ask what you can do for your country." But this is a line that translates well career-wise, too.

- *Trumpets his or her accomplishments—and the accomplishments of others.* It may seem ham-handed, even arrogant, but informing your boss and others of your successes and milestones is an important step toward visibility—and visibility does count. It's equally important to toot other people's horns occasionally. There is great power in a sincere compliment, and the favor invariably will be returned.

- *Stays ahead of the education curve.* Let's face it, we're in a global economy now where information is as much a commodity as compact disks or convertibles. Since technology changes seemingly on a daily basis, it is the savvy worker who keeps up. This could mean taking that class in Web design or simply chatting up your coworkers for the latest trends in commerce and technology. Think of this as business insurance.

- *Knows how to process feedback.* Listening is a lost art form and one that professionals who are serious about their careers should practice diligently. Therefore, make a vow to listen to what people at work are saying to you. You'll be surprised at how much you can learn about how people perceive you. Then work to make changes or—if the feedback is very positive— keep doing what you are doing. Also try to learn how to take feedback. If the feedback is positive, accept it by replying with a simple, "Thank you." If the feedback is negative, don't fly off the handle or take it personally. Instead, hear the person out. If you believe the feedback is not accurate, ask for examples. If you see it as legitimate, respond with appreciation for having this pointed out to you. If you disagree with it, calmly and confidently state your position. Don't argue or become upset.

- *Recognizes what he or she is worth.* Gold-collar workers always know their value to their company, to their industry, and to potential employers in myriad industries. There is no shortage of surveys and annual reports on salaries in the workplace. Check them out to see where someone of your experience and position stands. Another good idea is to scout out the help wanted ads (many include salary ranges these days) or contact an employment recruiter who's been around the block. Such a person can tell you what you're worth on the open market.

BECOMING A GOLD-COLLAR WORKER

There are other, more humanistic ways to separate gold-collar workers from the rest of the pack. Gold-collar workers seem to know who they are and how to relate to others. They know how to play office politics (more important, they know they *have* to play office politics to get ahead), and they know how to communicate with everyone in the workplace, from the intern in the mailroom to the company president.

In addition, gold-collar workers take workplace issues in stride. They know how to find something positive in every negative experience. Rather than feeling victimized over the fact that they didn't get a promotion, they focus on what they can learn from the situation. They may find that they need to brush up on their interview skills or polish up their résumés in preparation for a new job search. In this way, even a disappointment becomes a stepping-stone, not a roadblock.

Human relations are also a strong point of gold-collar workers. They learn to have compassion for both themselves and their fellow workers. If a big deadline is coming up fast and things are getting tense in close quarters, they don't take negative comments negatively, whether the comments were intended that way or not. If a comment is meant to hurt, then gold-collar workers don't want to give the sender the satisfaction of knowing that he hit his target. If the criticism is constructive, then gold-collar workers take it that way, filing the comment away in their minds and learning from the experience. Gold-collar workers also don't view their problems at work as unnatural or isolated. They realize that it is a natural part of the workplace to experience some negativity. In short, they use negativity to their advantage.

TRAITS THAT WILL INHIBIT YOUR BECOMING A GOLD-COLLAR WORKER: THE HOT DOG MAN

While a positive attitude is the foundation of a gold-collar worker's success, a negative one will just as surely reduce one's chances of moving up the career ladder. The funny thing is that most new employees have a great attitude coming into the workplace. But after being beaten down by office politics and inefficient management structures and strategies, many once-enthusiastic employees lose their enthusiasm. Cartoonist Scott Adams has made a nice little cottage industry out of this phenomenon with "Dilbert."

There's a parable about workplace influences on attitude called "The Man Who Sold Hot Dogs." In it, a 1930s-era man lives by the side of the road and sells hot dogs. He is hard of hearing, so he has no radio. He has no formal education, so he can't read. But he sells great hot dogs.

He spends his days standing at the side of the road hollering, "Buy a hot dog, mister?" And people do. So many do, in fact, that he doubles and then triples his bun and hot dog orders. He builds a nice roof for his stand so that people can eat his hot dogs in the rain or snow. He grows so busy that he calls on his son, recently home from college, to help out.

The son doesn't want any part of selling hot dogs, however. He tells his father, "Dad, don't you read the papers or listen to the radio? There's a war brewing in Europe, and we're in a recession at home. Things are terrible all over." Thinking the son, being a college graduate, must know what he is talking about, the man reduces his hot dog orders and pulls back on his bun deliveries. He takes down his roof and sells the spare parts. Soon he stops selling hot dogs by the side of the road altogether. Naturally, his bank account dwindles, and debts pile up in his mailbox.

The father says to his son, "You know son, you were right. We are in the middle of a great depression."

So don't let other people's negative attitudes poison your own. Keep your own course, and stay positive. Believe me, it will get you noticed.

WORKPLACE TYPES TO AVOID

There are some telltale workplace characteristics that will ensure that you never become a gold-collar worker (there's much more on this topic in Chapter 6). Slothfulness, dishonesty, undependability, and arrogance are traits that will ensure the unhappiness of the most ambitious career professional. Sure, such negative traits are obvious, and they likely don't apply to you. A closer look at some poor workplace habits of people you probably know, however, can help you avoid killing your career before you can accomplish the things you want:

- *The amateur.* Nobody likes an unprofessional worker, let alone wants to promote one. Moodiness, defensiveness, false pride, and ego have no place in the workplace. If your boss makes a decision that you deem foolish, keep it to yourself, and set out to complete your responsibilities with grace and good humor. Such an attitude will be received more glowingly than pouting about the ill-informed decision and then doing everything in your power to derail the project your boss just started.

- *The drifter.* Woody Allen once said that 90 percent of life was just showing up. This may be enough to keep a paycheck coming on a regular basis, but solid attendance without solid initiative is a recipe for career suicide. So if you demonstrate to your employers or to your fellow workers that you don't care about the company's latest press release or earnings report, you're also demonstrating your indifference to the company. At best, management will treat such an attitude with indifference in kind, probably resulting in mediocre performance reviews. At worst, management will treat your indifference as a slap in the face and go out of its way to block your progress inside the company.

- *The doormat.* Doormats are just as bad as drifters, if not worse. Someone who doesn't stick up for himself or doesn't go after opportunities rightfully sinks to the bottom of the workplace pecking order. Gold-collar workers are the antithesis of the doormat. They see promotion opportunities and grab them. Doormats don't shmooze, don't go to corporate functions—or sit quietly if they do go—don't make phone calls, and don't buttonhole other workers for information. In short, they don't assemble the data and credentials they can use later to cash in on career opportunities.

- *The rationalizer.* Rationalizers are those office types who start out fast, stall, and then ride out their careers like the drifter does, content to keep their middle-management positions and enjoy the meager benefits of their little fiefdoms. Rationalizers don't set goals, don't indulge in self-examination, and don't learn new skills. They are also among the earliest to lose their jobs when the pink slips start flying.

- *The disorganizer.* Disorganizers lose control over their own careers and often take others down with them. Sloppy work habits, inattention to detail, forgetfulness, and lack of focus are the hallmarks of the disorganizer. Disorganizers are notoriously poor communicators because they don't have their act together enough to discuss a project or workplace issue. This kicks off a domino effect as projects get delayed, timetables are ruined, product launches are pushed back, and morale suffers. Disorganizers are not prepared with the facts and dance around issues rather than dealing with them directly, and often they focus on people's reactions rather than the facts and the situation at hand. Disorganizers are career killers. Learn to stay away from them.

OTHER WAYS TO SINK YOUR CAREER PROSPECTS

Gold-collar workers don't have any of the preceding characteristics, and they don't make other career mistakes that can sink them faster than the iceberg that sunk the *Titanic*.

Gold-collar workers don't, for example, mix pleasure with business. While this includes not boozing it up at the office holiday party, it is not limited to the obvious stuff, such as carrying on a torrid affair in the workplace or drinking on the job. It is also the subtler stuff, such as spreading office gossip and "dissing" coworkers. This is not good. There was a saying in World War I that "loose lips sink ships," meaning that people who speak too freely might jeopardize a mission or, in the workplace, a project or someone's career.

Suffering from loose-lip syndrome can have a serious impact on your career. It could lead to your not being accepted by your peers, which in turn severely limits how effective you can be on the job. It also can lead to criticism from your boss—the last thing you want to hear from the person who—besides you—has the most influence on your career.

Sometimes workplace confrontations can't be helped, no matter who's at fault. When people work together for long periods of time, often in close quarters, raw feelings, misunderstandings, and harsh words are inevitable. If you are mistreated at work, you'll be tempted to get even. But be careful: Making enemies can lead straight to job misery. Even if you have been treated unfairly, you can take the high road. While practicing forgiveness may be the last thing you want to do, it is often the wisest move.

Overall, a gold-collar worker will conduct a self-examination of his or her workplace interaction skills. Gold-collar workers ask themselves how well they get along with their peers and supervisors. Do they frequently find themselves at odds with others? Do they spew out their aggressions in front of coworkers or behind their backs? The ability to get along with others is a key success factor in the workplace. A lack of emotional maturity in this area can limit even those with the highest intellect and best work aptitude. If any of these traits or experiences apply to you, consider this a big career red flag.

REALITY CHECK: PATH TO ENTREPRENEURSHIP FILLED WITH SMALL BUSINESS EXPERIENCES

Ask an entrepreneur how he or she got started, and invariably you'll hear about treating your corporate career as your own small business.

Treating your job as if it were a small business and you were the owner is a key ingredient to long-term career success, whether you wind up starting your own home business or moving on up the corporate ladder.

Take Sharon Reilly, one-time stay-at-home mother to a pair of fine young boys and now the owner of her own small grocery store in Cape Cod, Massachusetts. It's a cozy shop where sunburnt customers stop in to get anything from a six-pack of beer to freshly baked bagels and muffins. Before having children, Reilly spent six years working for a local computer company in the customer service department. There, she learned that the trick to succeeding in the customer care game was to act as if she owned the business and those were her customers on the line.

"When my phone would ring, it became easy for me to put myself in my customer's shoes," says the energetic 44-year-old entrepreneur. "If the software we sold the customer wasn't working or wasn't delivered on time, I took it personally and gave hell to the person on our end who was responsible. I made sure that the customer got satisfaction, just as I do now at my store."

Reilly learned that there's no better experience for running your own business than to have *practiced* running your own business. Even if it means doing so with someone else's company.

3

"Are Those Swim Trunks You're Wearing, Fishbein?" Understanding Corporate Culture

Find a job you love and add five days to every week.

This is easier said than done, right?

One way to find a job and a career you love is by identifying early on the corporate culture of the firm that employs you. Ideally, you'd like to accomplish this before you climb aboard, but even if you can't, you'll benefit from knowing your company's culture and adapting to it no matter how long you've been with the company.

HOW DO YOU DEFINE CORPORATE CULTURE?

Not so easily, I'm afraid, because every company's founder or chief executive officer (CEO) might provide her own definition. In wholesale terms, corporate culture means developing a core set of assumptions, understandings, and implicit rules that govern day-to-day behavior in the workplace. These concepts taken together generally are known as *organizational,* or *corporate, culture* because they provide a blueprint of the internal environment of major corporations. Corporate culture, by definition, is also a system of shared values, assumptions, beliefs, and norms that unite the employees of a given company. Corporate culture aligns employee behavior, develops organizational commitment, and provides social workplace guidelines.

This is a definition of corporate culture that is derived from a theoretical background. In practice, identifying corporate culture at the place you work can be a bit easier to accomplish. That's because over time companies, intentionally or not, develop their own cultures.

Some companies, for example, are easily identifiable by their penchant for secrecy. Consider IBM, the poster child for corporate paranoia. When Microsoft was tapped by "Big Blue" to develop the operating system for the IBM personal computer back in the late 1970s, it required extraordinary security measures from the then miniscule but laid-back startup in Redmond, Washington. First, the room where the project was being developed had to be windowless, unventilated, and locked at all times. IBM sent its own file locks, and when Microsoft founder Bill Gates had trouble installing them, IBM sent its own expert installer. Gates grew used to it as a small army of IBM workers dropped by continuously to check up on Microsoft.

When Gates and company finished the project (and thus paved the way for Microsoft's industry dominance), IBM didn't acknowledge Microsoft's contribution directly. Instead, it sent a "Dear Vendor" form letter notifying Gates that the job was done to the satisfaction of IBM (which, to its credit, IBM apologized to Gates for sending).

Other companies are identified by the way they reflect their leaders. When Wal-Mart was just starting out, founder Sam Walton visited a tennis ball factory in South Korea where workers kicked off each day with group calisthenics and a company cheer. Impressed by what he called the "whistle while you work philosophy," Walton instituted the Wal-Mart corporate cheer, which now begins every morning meeting at Wal-Mart stores across the country. This none too subtle form of cultural reinforcement encourages enthusiasm for the company and reminds sales associates of the need to focus on customer satisfaction.

Other companies like to emphasize responsibility and accountability—two great character traits for employees to emulate. At one memorable annual meeting, Doug Burgum, CEO of Great Plains, smashed three eggs on his head in front of employees and industry partners after releasing a product with performance problems. Burgum made it clear that he took a large part of the responsibility for the egg on his company's face.

WHY A CORPORATE CULTURE ANYWAY?

Companies like to instill corporate culture in their workers for a variety of reasons. One reason, as you'll see in a moment, is to keep employees from leaving the company. Another key reason is to encourage employees to demonstrate an understanding and enthusiasm for their company. At Atlanta-based Home Depot, new employees, even executives, spend two weeks working on the sales floor, learning what customers want and need and receiving a ground-zero view of the company's core business. In the stores, employees also rub shoulders with Home Depot's customer base of do-it-yourselfers, whose entrepreneurial spirit the company has deliberately tried to build into its corporate culture. To promote teamwork—and to get an up-close view of how its products are being used and to what effect— Home Depot also encourages employees to participate in organized local community building efforts such as Habitat for Humanity's house-building projects and has helped repair a run-down school.

Corporate culture can be industry-specific as well. IBM aside, the risk-taking and dress-casual work environments of the typical Silicon Valley software company often reflect the entrepreneurial, if laid-back, lifestyles of the company founders. You know, people like Bill Gates or Apple Computer's Steve Jobs.

Three thousand miles across the country on Wall Street, financial services companies encourage a different type of corporate culture that reinforces the seriousness of their tasks. Taking care of people's money is sober business, so banks and brokerage companies look to instill ethical mindsets that tell customers that their money is in safe hands. The object there is to look professional. For example, Wall Street—along with the legal services industry—was one of the last sectors to fall into line with casual dress codes. Even today, many banks and insurance firms don't allow casual dress in the office. And of the ones that do, corporate culture is so ingrained that brokers and bankers often choose to wear standard business attire anyway. After all, who wants to give their money to a guy wearing Bermuda shorts?

MORE THAN MEETS THE EYE

Emphasizing a corporate culture is far more than offering not-so-subtle reminders to zip one's lip (as at IBM), champion customer service (as at Wal-Mart), become civic-minded (as at Home Depot), or encourage a stand-up attitude (as at Great Plains). It is also a savvy bottom-line-oriented business strategy designed to sell more widgets, attract new customers, and keep employees from leaving the company (and avoid incurring costly rehiring and retraining costs). While every company wants to sell more products and snag more customers, the true bottom-line benefit of a corporate culture is in keeping employees on board with little or no thought of jumping ship.

Think about it. Reducing net turnover by 3 percent (in a company with 40,000 employees) translates into 1000 employees per year who do not have to be recruited, hired, and trained—which adds up to a savings of million of dollars in overall costs. Smart companies that actively promote their corporate cultures know that environment and culture are the strongest reasons why people stay with a company.

CORPORATE CULTURE CAN GO TOO FAR

Some companies can take corporate culture too seriously and harm themselves in the process. One lighter example of this involves British publishing tycoon Robert Maxwell. This publishing giant hated smoking and forbade it in his workplace.

One day he walked by the mailroom and saw a man puffing away. Maxwell immediately got in the unfortunate man's face and reminded him that the penalty for smoking was termination. "How much do you earn?" asked Maxwell.

"Seventy-five pounds a week," answered the smoker.

Maxwell reached into his wallet and took out four weeks' worth of cash and handed it to the man. "Here's one month's severance. You're fired," he huffed. The man took the money and promptly left. What Maxwell didn't know until a secretary informed him minutes later was that the smoker wasn't an employee of the firm. He was simply visiting a mail-room employee.

The lesson? Instituting a corporate culture is laudable, but you can easily overdo it.

HOW TO IDENTIFY YOUR COMPANY'S CULTURE

Not knowing your company's cultural tendencies—or worse, knowing them and ignoring them—can be harmful to your career. Back in 1985, a U.S. district court judge ruled that American Airlines had the right to fire a customer services clerk for not smiling. The clerk's lawyer had argued that the employee had met every requirement of the job save for the smile. But the judge ruled that the airline's policy of requiring a friendly smile was critical in the competitive airline industry. The employee lost the argument—and his job—for disregarding—or worse, not knowing—a core component of his company's culture.

How well do you know your own company's culture? Could you describe it to an outsider? Could you, in 10 words or less, describe what's really important at your company? Who gets promoted and why? What employee behaviors get rewarded? In short, could you pass your firm's version of the "smile test"?

If you can't, you're in good company. The fact is that despite management's best efforts, not many employees know what their company's corporate culture is or if it even has one.

As the hapless customer services clerk at American Airlines discovered, however, corporate culture has a direct effect on the people an organization employs. In fact, an argument can be made that the culture of an organization affects the types of people employed, their career aspirations, their educational backgrounds, and their status in society. This is so because the culture of a company can either embrace or reject people—people who either fit in with a company's culture or do not.

This is why it is a good idea to recognize your company's culture as soon as possible.

This shouldn't be so tough for someone who's already survived the rigors of multiple job interviews and the agonies of providing personal references to land the job in the first place. In fact, most job candidates have researched their potential employer already from many angles: organizational viability, management's expectations, opportunities for growth, and competitive compensation.

Gauging your company's workplace culture isn't as obvious as checking its quarterly returns for the past eight quarters. Here, subtlety is the ticket. Therefore, don't go barging into the next marketing meeting and ham-handedly demand to know what makes your company tick. You'll no doubt be escorted from the room by your lower lip, likely by a security guard named Bruno.

Instead, pay attention to specific clues that give your company's self-image away. Do this while you go about your business. Here's a list of ways you can stealthily but effectively discern your company's culture:

Study the Manner in Which Information Is Exchanged

Remember that marketing meeting? Next time you go to one—or to any corporate meeting, social event, or water-cooler banter session—listen and listen well. Take note of how people talk about the company. Do they puff up and champion their company's self-image? Do they reference it in mocking tones? Or not at all? A sign that a company has a good culture is if people say *we* a lot instead of *the company* (as in,

"We're going with vendor A instead of vendor B because it is civic-minded, enthusiastic, and customer-service-driven like we are"). A big red flag should be apparent when staff-level employees show no inclination that they know of a particular corporate culture, let alone want to talk about one.

How Are Assignments Handed Out?

Are assignments at your firm handed out with crisp, clear, and compelling directions? Or is it a "sink or swim" deal where instructions are vague and directions to data are confusing? If the former situation is the norm, then it appears that your company isn't one to play games and check you out using subterfuge. Companies that impose assignments or deadlines on personnel, especially new personnel, without clear directions may be testing their personnel to see how well they can cope on their own. Chances are that this is a company that not only will play games with you but also doesn't have a positive corporate culture.

How Is Big News Relayed at Your Company?

Companies' information delivery methods also will mirror their cultural tendencies. This is especially true when big news is in the offing on a new merger or potential job cuts. A company that uses e-mail or, God forbid, a company newsletter to deliver big news probably fosters a cold and impersonal corporate culture. Either that or it's hiding something and doesn't want to answer any questions. A company that gathers its employees in the cafeteria or off-site location or has its managers deliver the news face to face in a one-on-one format, however, cares about how the news will affect its employees. It is saying that it's okay to ask questions of management in the flesh, so to speak, and that the most important issue is how the news affects employees. This is a company that has a nice corporate culture.

What Kinds of Questions Were You Asked at Your Job Interview?

You may have been too nervous to remember, but recalling the line of questioning during your job interview can go a long way toward determining your company's corporate culture. If the questions were more results-oriented (such as "What was your most challenging project at your last job?"), then chances are that you're working for a company that embraces the bottom line. This is not a bad thing— just be prepared to demonstrate the work ethic your employer likely is looking for. If the line of questioning ran more along the lines of, say, "Where are you going in your career, and what hobbies do you have?" then this company likely emphasizes more of an employee-satisfaction work culture and might be a bit easier to work for. Of course, don't forget that such a company has a bottom line, too.

If you're in the process of interviewing for a new job, use the job interview to understand the company's culture. Ask such questions as

- How would you describe the nature of the work environment?
- How do you think managers within the company would describe their management philosophies or roles?
- Do you feel that you know what is expected of you?
- Do you receive feedback on your performance?
- Are there opportunities for development and training?

The answers to these questions will provide you with a road map for your career whether you wind up working for the company or not.

What Does Your Company Say About Itself?

How your company positions itself in its own marketing materials is a good way to get at the essence of its corporate image. Open an annual report and see the term *results-oriented* a few times, and there's a good chance you're working for a tough cookie of a company. The same goes for *mission-oriented* and *bottom-line-driven.* But if you see such terms as *entrepreneurial* and *family atmosphere,* you are probably with a firm that prides itself on keeping its employees as happy as it does its shareholders.

Aquarium or Foosball?

The way a company is laid out is another key to determining corporate culture. The next time you go to work, take a longer look at your company's reception area. Does it have an aquarium or a van Gogh-like still life hanging on the wall? Or does it have a wall full of framed press clippings and a Foosball table nearby? What kind of music is playing, if any? Mozart or Mellencamp? A sober, more sedate front office will be clean, almost Spartan. It might have a tasteful Renoir clone on the wall but not much more than that. The receptionist will be polished and cleancut. The aura here is order and organization. This is not a bad place to be for employees who place a high priority on order and organization. But a front office with some Grateful Dead album covers on the wall and a receptionist with a diamond stud pierced through his lip—if there's a receptionist at all—is sending a completely different message. It is saying, "We're busy, and we don't have much of a hierarchy, so come on in and roll your sleeves up and help us get our new product out on time." Again, this is not a bad place to be if you're looking to make your mark quickly and can survive, or thrive, in a free-form work environment.

Ask an Ex-Employee

This one is just about foolproof. Sooner or later you're going to run into someone who used to work at your company—maybe even in your old job. You'll be at a local watering hole, and a friend of a coworker will drop by and mention that, yep, he once worked at your company too. Take advantage of this situation, but do so diplomatically. If the person was fired for letting a rabid weasel loose in the chief financial officer's (CFO's) office, then he probably is not a good candidate for usable information (although such a person may be a good candidate for shock therapy). More likely, your new friend is a reasonable sort who left the company reluctantly but who had a better job offer down the road. This happens all the time. So squeeze next to this person and politely ask what he thought of the company, what its strengths and weaknesses are, how management solved problems, and how happy he was at the firm. Depending on how many beers you quaffed while prying this information out of the ex-employee, you should soon have a fairly objective and candid view of what your company is all about, self-image and more.

Did You Ever Get a Job Description?

Companies that hand you a sturdy, clearly defined job description invariably place a greater emphasis on individuals and how one employee can make a big difference on his own. Such companies are saying, "While you may work as part of a team here, we're depending on you and you alone to handle these tasks." Companies that don't deliver job descriptions to the newly hired or newly promoted tend to emphasize a workgroup office culture where titles are meaningless and individuals are expected to wear many different hats. There's more of an emphasis on being a jack-of-all-trades rather than the master of one.

There's nothing wrong with this approach as long as you recognize it and see yourself as a jack-of-all-trades.

Conflict or Harmony

Remember Digital Equipment Corporation? In the 1960s, 1970s, and 1980s, founder Kenneth Olsen built one of the most successful computer companies in the world. Part of his blueprint was building an organizational matrix that fostered competition between departments. His thinking was that by pairing departments off against each other, the more innovative, committed department invariably would wrestle the best projects and assignments away. This, in turn, would lead to the product being developed (theoretically) by the best people. Companies that promote conflict have corporate cultures that may not appeal to quiet, introspective people. Such people may fare better at companies that emphasize harmony over competition. But if you like raw meat for breakfast, companies like Digital are just what the doctor ordered.

What's Your Pay, Pal?

Usually, when individuals start a new job, companies pay them the minimum salary for that job. "Prove yourself first, and then we will give you a raise" is the accepted practice. This conservative approach promotes a plodding, cautious work style. In the Internet era, a more progressive philosophy toward reward is needed to encourage leaps in learning and more risk taking. One incentive is to pay individuals generously up front and hold them to a higher standard of performance that can only be achieved by daring to do things differently. It says, "Although you may not have the experience, we think that you have

the potential, so we will pay you in line with the full value of the job."
If this is the case, though, expect to spend a great deal of time proving yourself over and over again. Late hours often may be in the mix. In short, this is a close cousin of the conflict workplace strategy.

Owners or Not?

Companies that like to throw around the words *employees* and *owners* in the same sentence are likely trying to create an entrepreneurial corporate culture where everybody has a legitimate stake in the company's fortunes. Such companies are saying that owners are people who step out from behind titles and job descriptions to act on behalf of customers and the company. Nonowners hide behind position descriptions ("It's not my job") and throw problems over functional walls ("Let me transfer you to . . .") as excuses for inaction. Owners focus on the business results of their actions regardless of who's watching. Nonowners focus on the chain of command. So, if it's action and risk a-plenty you desire, then it's the owner route for you. If it's safety ye be seeking, then . . .

Do You See the Big Picture?

Companies with customer-service-driven cultures often take great pains to show employees how their actions—or inactions—can set off a chain of events that can help or hurt the company. At Southwest Airlines, for example, gate agents are reminded that when they push a plane just 30 seconds late, that delay could translate into 1 hour and 45 minutes at the end of 11 flights in a day. Southwest would have to add 35 more planes at $30 million each to maintain its schedule. This could mean wage concessions, profit sharing, and lower job security. Southwest's gate agents know how their job performance creates results and how those results affect their lives. Customer-service-cultured companies often make information relevant and interesting to their employees.

How Employee Friendly Is Your Employee-Friendly Company?

Does your company walk the talk when it comes to touting its employee-friendly workplace. If so, then such perks as good health and dental plans, onsite childcare, and onsite fitness centers should be yours for the asking. Try not to make too much of perks as part of a larger corporate culture, though. Some companies offer these perks to keep you onsite well past the dinner hour. While this may be fine for a 23-year-old singleton, a working mother might not appreciate any efforts to keep her from away from her home. What well-configured perks will do is promote loyalty, and this in and of itself is a corporate culture, too.

Who Do You Love?

The most important thing to remember when examining a company's corporate culture is that corporate cultures are not one size fits all; the effectiveness of a given culture depends on the company's business goals. Some companies take decades of trial and error before their culture pays off in terms of employee retention, a good public image, and higher revenues. Companies that try to get away with sticking a label on themselves as "employee friendly" or "entrepreneurial" without putting in the time needed to merit the label usually wind up with a culture of indecision, if not deceit.

Therefore, put a great deal of effort into determining your company's corporate culture—or finding out the culture of a company you may wind up working for. Knowing how to determine a company's culture and finding a company with a culture that's right for you constitute a ticket to a promising and profitable career.

ORGANIZATIONAL CULTURE AND YOUR COMPATIBILITY: A TEST

Here's a handy test for determining a company's corporate culture. Just answer these questions using the choices following each. The score for each answer choice follows in parentheses. Total up all your answers.

Leadership

1. How much confidence do managers seem to have in employees?

   ___ Don't know (0); ___ No confidence (1); ___ Little confidence (5); ___ Substantial confidence (10); ___ Complete confidence (15)

2. Do employees feel free to talk to managers about their jobs?

   ___ Don't know (0); ___ Not at all (1); ___ Not very (5); ___ Rather free (10); ___ Fully free (15)

3. Are employees' ideas sought out and used, if worthy?

   ___ Don't know (0); ___ Seldom (1); ___ Sometimes (5); ___ Usually (10); ___ Always (15)

Motivation

4. How predominantly does management use fear, threats, punishment, rewards, and/or involvement?

___ Don't know (0); ___ Mostly fear, threats, and punishment with occasional rewards (1); ___ Rewards and some punishment (5); ___ Rewards, some punishment, and some involvement (10); ___ Primarily rewards and involvement based on goals set by the group (15)

5. Where is responsibility placed for achieving organization's goals?

___ Don't know (0); ___ Mostly at the top (1); ___ Top and middle managers (5); ___ Generally throughout the company (10); ___ At all levels (15)

Communication

6. How much communication is devoted to achieving the organization's objectives?

___ Don't know (0); ___ Very little (1); ___ Little (5); ___ Quite a bit (10); ___ A great deal (15)

7. How does information flow within the company?

___ Don't know (0); ___ Top down (1); ___ Mostly top down (5); ___ Down and up (10); ___ Down, up, and sideways (15)

8. How is top-down communication accepted?

___ Don't know (0); ___ With suspicion (1); ___ Possibly with suspicion (5); ___ With caution (10); ___ With an open mind (15)

9. How accurate is upward communication?

___ Don't know (0); ___ Often wrong (1); ___ Censored for boss (5); ___ Limited accuracy (10); ___ Accurate (15)

10. How well do managers know and really understand the problems faced by employees?

___ Don't know (0); ___ Very little knowledge or understanding (1); ___ Some knowledge (5); ___ Understand well (10); ___ Understand very well (15)

Decision Making

11. At what level are decisions made?

___ Don't know (0); ___ Mostly at the top level (1); ___ Policy at the top levels, some delegation (5); ___ Broad policy at the top, more delegation (10); ___ Decisions made throughout, well integrated with overall organization goals (15)

12. Where does the technical and professional knowledge used in decision making originate?

___ Don't know (0); ___ Top management (1); ___ Upper and middle management (5); ___ To a certain extent throughout the organization (10); ___ To a great deal throughout the organization (15)

13. How much are employees involved in decisions related to and affecting their work?

___ Don't know (0); ___ Not at all (1); ___ Occasionally consulted (5); ___ Generally consulted (10); ___ Fully involved (15)

14. What does the decision-making process contribute to motivation?

___ Don't know (0); ___ Usually nothing (1); ___ Relatively little or weakens motivation (5); ___ Some contribution (10); ___ Substantial contribution (15)

Organization's Goals

15. How are organizational goals established?

    ___ Don't know (0); ___ Orders issued (1); ___ Mostly by orders, with some comment invited (5); ___ Orders issued after discussion (10); ___ Primarily by group action (15)

16. How much covert resistance to goals is present?

    ___ Don't know (0); ___ Strong resistance (1); ___ Moderate resistance (5); ___ Some resistance at times (10); ___ Little or none (15)

Control Issues

17. Is there an informal organization resisting the formal organization?

    ___ Don't know (0); ___ Yes (1); ___ Usually (5); ___ Sometimes (10); ___ No, they share the same goals (15)

18. How are cost, productivity, and other control data used?

    ___ Don't know (0); ___ Policing and punishment (1); ___ Reward and punishment (5); ___ Reward and some self-guidance (10); ___ Self-guidance and problem solving (15)

19. How much cooperative teamwork exists?

    ___ Don't know (0); ___ None (1); ___ Little (5); ___ Some (10); ___ A great deal (15)

20. What is the overall context of the corporate culture?

    ___ Don't know (0); ___ Sick, toxic, unhealthy, stifling, and hostile (1); ___ Overly bureaucratic but not hostile (5); ___ Working to improve productivity (10); ___ Great place to work! (15)

Scoring the Results

The higher the score, the healthier is the organizational culture (in my opinion).

Total Under 100
The company is not taking advantage of employee contributions, ideas, and energy. The company may be experimenting with restructuring, downsizing, or reengineering, or it may still be trapped by overly bureaucratic procedures.

Total 101–200
The company probably is trying to improve communication and productivity; there may be departments and divisions that work very well and others that don't work as well.

Total 201–300
The company is productive, and most people like working there, even though there may still be areas where things are not ideal.

REALITY CHECK: CULTURE SHOCK

There's an old adage about how difficult it is to place a round block into a square hole.

Two-year-olds understand this, though it doesn't stop them from trying when they're playing with blocks and puzzles. They just grow frustrated.

So too do career-minded professionals who find themselves working for companies where they don't seem to "fit in."

That's what happened to Michael Flaherty, now a 30-something success story with a senior vice-presidency at a national insurance firm. But when the shy, bookish type who preferred ballet to baseball started out, he was hired by a major Wall Street brokerage firm as an analyst. Eager to pore over company records and unearth some great stocks for the firm's clients, he found himself at sea in a rowdy corporate culture where employees were expected to go out for drinks every night and mingle with the firm's customers. During work hours, the air turned blue with obscenities as traders and brokers lost money in the stock market.

It was a chaotic workplace environment, and Flaherty did his best to assimilate. But within a year he gave up the job and went to work for an insurance firm that marketed variable annuities to customers—a workplace where an atmosphere of calm prevailed and where he was much happier.

"Looking back, I wish that I'd done some due diligence and found out what it was like to actually work at a place like my old brokerage firm," he recalls. "I had friends who'd had the experience and warned me about it, but I didn't want to listen. I was blinded a bit by the money and the challenges of working on Wall Street. I found out too late it wasn't for me."

Flaherty quickly recognized that, while money and prestige are alluring reasons to work for a company, if it is a company that doesn't fit your personality, everything else becomes secondary.

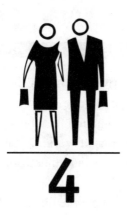

4

Easy Ways to Derail Your Career

To paraphrase political humorist Finley Peter Dunne's Mr. Dooley, career advancement ain't beanbag. All Mr. Dunne is saying is that politics, like the workplace, is no place for the thin-skinned and the shirkers. You've got to produce, and you have to be prepared to wear your work ethic on your shoulder.

No question about it, throughout your career, you are going to be judged by others—bosses, coworkers, and clients—about which kind of person you are—a "lifter" or a "leaner."

The answer goes a long way in determining how successful your career will be and how happy you will be with your life. President John F. Kennedy was thinking of lifters and leaners when he famously told Americans, "Ask not what your country can do for you, ask what you can do for your country." In other words, society doesn't owe you a living. In fact, you owe society the best effort you can give.

Don't be the person who believes that your parents, the government, a corporation, or anyone else owes you a living. The person who thinks that he can gain a livelihood without hard work will wake up one day to find himself working for another person who felt that nobody owed him a living and therefore earned the right to have others work for him.

Companies don't want people like this. In fact, they'll go out of their way to get rid of leaners. The good news is that they'll also go out of their way to reward lifters.

ARE YOU A LIFTER OR A LEANER?

It's easy to separate lifters from leaners:

The lifter is always a part of the answer.
The leaner is always a part of the problem.

The lifter always has a program.
The leaner always has an excuse.

The lifter says, "Let me do it for you."
The leaner says, "That's not my job."

The lifter sees an answer for every problem.
The leaner sees a problem in every answer.

The lifter says, "It may be difficult, but it's possible."
The leaner says, "It may be possible, but it's too difficult."

This chapter isn't about lifters—it's about leaners. Sure, I'd rather spend time talking about how to achieve and get ahead—after all, this is what this book is about. But part of achieving is recognizing the kinds of things that can keep you from achieving.

Things like tardiness, unkempt appearance, surliness to your coworkers and customers, passivity, and more. These are at the top of the list of things that can ruin your career. Not only that—they can get you fired, too.

A LIST OF THE TOP 9 THINGS THAT CAN GET YOU FIRED

Since you are reading this book and possess the initiative to try to get ahead in the workplace and in your career, you likely don't possess any of the following negative workplace characteristics, each of which can get you pink-slipped in a hurry. But read on to make sure.

Poor Work Quality

Shoddy performance in the workplace, whether it's putting on a fan belt backward or carelessly sticking wrong numbers into an annual report, is public enemy number 1 to management. Not only can mistakes and errors have an impact on the bottom line, they also can reduce morale in the company's rank and file. This is not to confuse poor quality with the determined and innovative worker who makes mistakes. Henry Ford forgot to put a reverse gear in his first car, and Thomas Edison once spent $2 million on an invention that never saw the light of day. Good workers make mistakes. Bad ones keep repeating them.

Poor Customer Service

In client-driven corporate environments, such as at an advertising agency or a car dealership, mishandling customers is an obvious no-no. We've all waited in line at a store while a clerk chats on the phone to a friend. In more sophisticated workplaces, however, things like not returning client phone calls or disregarding a complaint and taking no action on it are just as bad. Any CEO worth his or her salt will tell you that in business, the customer is king.

Dishonesty

Stealing a stapler from the company is bad, but lying to coworkers or to management is worse. Employers will quickly jettison employees they can't trust to tell the truth.

Undependability

If you develop a pattern of not finishing assignments or calling in sick too often, you can start counting the days until you're fired in double-digits. Like a football coach who cuts a quarterback because he can't get him out of the trainer's room, a corporate manager will lobby hard for an employee's dismissal if he can't count on the employee's help. Having a cavalier attitude about it doesn't help either. There's the story about the employee who called in sick once. Her boss told her, "You didn't look sick when I saw you at the local pub last night." She answered, "You should have seen me after the fourth martini." Not good!

Lack of Respect

Showing disrespect not only to managers but also to coworkers, clients, and business partners is a fast way to get yourself canned. Ignoring a coworker's repeated e-mails about a project, blowing off meetings run by a different department head, and mouthing off to a client who has a problem are good examples of how disrespect can have you checking out the Help Wanted pages with sudden urgency.

Chronic Lateness

I mentioned earlier in this book that Woody Allen once said that 90 percent of life was just showing up. Preferably, you also want to do this *on time.* Not doing so is not being dependable.

Sexual Harassment

Professionals who aren't careful about how they treat their coworkers can find themselves out on the street with a badly damaged reputation. This is what spreading an ill-advised joke around the office or making an off-color remark to a coworker can do to you. In the workplace, keep the dirty jokes and disparaging remarks to yourself.

Socializing

Over the past few decades, the workplace has become a de facto social setting where coworkers sometimes pair off and embark on torrid workplace relationships. In and of itself, this is not a bad thing (the seeds of many a great marriage were planted in the workplace). But a relationship with a married coworker or an affair with a supervisor or manager can end disastrously in terms of both romance and your career. Many professionals see their careers sidetracked by office romances, with a departure from the company a common result.

Stealing

Theft is a crime in any U.S. state. Therefore, whether it's lifting computer software from your office desktop or embezzling checks from your company, stealing is never tolerated and virtually always punished with dismissal and, often, criminal charges. William F. James, the founder of Boys Town, once said that there were three ingredients to success: normal intelligence, determination, and honesty. Of the latter, he added that one cannot be a little bit dishonest—it's all the way or nothing.

MORE CAREER STOPPERS

As I said, I doubt anyone reading this book is doing these things. At least, I hope not. What's more probable are the subtle things you can do professionally that you don't even realize can slow or stop your career growth. These include such things as screwing up in a job interview or gossiping about a coworker. These and other character traits, personality quirks, and dubious workplace habits can place you into a career pickle very quickly.

Let's take a closer look at them.

Bad Résumés and Cover Letters

Stalled careers often get early starts. In fact, some careers can be derailed right out of the gate by bad résumés and poor cover letters. Human resources professionals call them *bad first impressions*. They do so with good reason.

The following include some of the most common résumé mistakes. Learn to avoid them when updating your résumé.

It's All About You

Employers would rather run their businesses than read your résumé. Therefore, yours must quickly answer the question on every employer's mind: "What can you do for me?"

The problem with many résumés is that they begin with the premise, "What can you do for me?" Such phrases as "Seeking a position with potential for career advancement" or "Manager looking for position with more financial opportunities" will find a manager's circular file and quickly.

A good résumé starts out with the notion that you can help a company rather than that a company should help you. Emphasize early on how you can contribute to the company's bottom line or how your sales, marketing, and management experience will add to profitability.

Generic Blathering

My idea of hell would be reading résumés that include mundane phrases like "responsibilities included . . ." or "I implemented policies and procedures." What busy manager wants to read this?

It's okay, even advisable, to talk yourself up on your résumé. This is why résumés exist in the first place. Instead of tossing banal generalities at hiring managers, however, be more specific. Instead of saying "I was responsible for shipping and handling," say "I helped increase product turnover by 20 percent and sales by 15 percent in five months."

Some hiring managers are going to pound their desks and say, "I could use a go-getter like that!" But if you insist on sticking to generic phrases, hiring managers are more likely to say, "I could use some aspirin" instead.

Typo Terrorists

Aye carumba! The Holy Grail of bad résumés is bad spelling. Nothing will get your résumé deep-sixed faster than spelling the name of the hiring manager or the name of the company to which you are applying wrong. Even general terms like *receive* ("recieve") or *Bachelor of Arts* ("Bacheler of Arts") are easy to misspell if you're not paying attention.

To avoid being a typo terrorist, proofread your résumé three times: once for accuracy (numbers, dates, city names, etc.), once for missing or extra words, and once more for spelling. Then read it backward to look for weird spacings or punctuation.

Poor Packaging

Some résumés resemble wedding invitations more than they do business correspondence. Two or maybe three fonts with a mix of boldface and italics and underlines are not uncommon. Worse might be the résumé with a type so tiny that the hiring manager needs a magnifying glass to read it. One friend of mine was bragging about his great résumé that was sure to get management's attention. His strategy? He capitalized every word. When I told him his résumé looked more like a ransom note or a used car ad, he called me narrow-minded. The last I heard, he was still looking for work.

Résumé Blunders

Below are some real résumés chronicled in the July 21, 1997 issue of *Fortune* magazine that could have made hiring managers both laugh and cry. I can only assume that the applicants didn't make the first interview.

1. "I demand a salary commiserate with my extensive experience."
2. "I have lurnt Word Perfect 6.0 computor and spreadsheet progroms."
3. "Received a plague for Salesperson of the Year."
4. "Reason for leaving last job: maturity leave."
5. "Wholly responsible for two (2) failed financial institutions."
6. "Failed bar exam with relatively high grades."

7. "It's best for employers that I not work with people."

8. "Let's meet, so you can 'ooh' and 'aah' over my experience."

9. "You will want me to be Head Honcho in no time."

10. "Am a perfectionist and rarely if if ever forget details."

11. "I was working for my mom until she decided to move."

12. "Marital status: Single. Unmarried. Unengaged. Uninvolved. No commitments."

13. "I have an excellent track record, although I am not a horse."

14. "I am loyal to my employer at all costs. . . . Please feel free to respond to my résumé on my office voice mail."

15. "I have become completely paranoid, trusting completely no one and absolutely nothing."

16. "My goal is to be a meteorologist. But since I possess no training in meteorology, I suppose I should try stock brokerage."

17. "I procrastinate, especially when the task is unpleasant."

18. "As indicted, I have over five years of analyzing investments."

19. "Personal interests: Donating blood. Fourteen gallons so far."

20. "Instrumental in ruining entire operation for a Midwest chain store."

21. "Note: Please don't miscontrue my 14 jobs as 'job-hopping.' I have never quit a job."

22. "Marital status: often. Children: various."

23. "Reason for leaving last job: They insisted that all employees get to work by 8:45 a.m. every morning. Could not work under those conditions."

24. "The company made me a scapegoat, just like my three previous employers."

25. "Finished eighth in my class of ten."

26. "References: None. I've left a path of destruction behind me."

Job Interview Gaffes

My sympathies go out to the army of nervous, anxious job seekers trembling in human resources department waiting rooms as we speak. It is not easy selling yourself to a company, especially in a gut-wrenching one-on-one interview process that would make the Marquis de Sade wince.

No matter how many goose bumps you get or how jangled your nerves are, the show must go on. When you do get the green light for a job interview, try to ensure that the process avoids the following mistakes—any one of which can sink your job chances.

Showing Up Late

Whatever you do, show up on time. You'll know you left a hiring manager waiting too long when you see steam coming from under her door before you rush in—steam from her ears. Besides the fact that it's rude and that you won't be on your game if you stagger in all heart-pounding, sweaty, and late, showing up late for an interview is a good way to demonstrate that your dependability leaves much to be desired. Thus, when you get the call or the e-mail signaling that the interview is a go, respond right back showing your appreciation for the opportunity. Then make sure you get easy directions to the company. Consider buying a map or using one of the many Internet maps that can pinpoint an address for you (Maps.com is good). Also wear a watch and leave early. If the worst happens and you can't make it on time, call the interviewer and arrange to reschedule. One last point: Try not to show up too early either. Sitting in a waiting room for two hours won't help you get a job, and it'll likely irritate the people you're trying to win over.

Poor Dress Habits

Some well-intentioned job applicants can't seem to tell the difference between a job interview and happy hour at the Bongo Room. Studies show that you make the greatest impact on the interviewer in the first 17 seconds. God forbid that the impression you make should be Madonna circa 1985 or Jethro Bodine from *The Beverly Hillbillies*. Therefore, dress conservatively, in subdued colors, and wear little or no jewelry. Shoes should be low-heeled and polished. Hygiene is key—combed hair, brushed teeth, deodorant, and low-key scent. Arrive early and use the restroom just before the interview.

Poor Due Diligence

Wall Street types use the term *due diligence* a lot. It means doing research on a company before you sink money into it. Job interview candidates would do well to conduct their own due diligence campaign. Take the time beforehand to investigate the company's products and services, annual sales, structure, and other key information (much of which is available on the Internet). Or go to the public library, read professional magazines, or seek out former employees. Remember, there's a big difference between asking about a company's stock price and telling a manager why it's priced where it is during a job interview. In the job interview game, askers are shown the door. Tellers are shown job offers.

Lousy Conversation Habits

Rambling may be a good tendency if you're a fullback for the Pittsburgh Steelers, but it's a lousy one when you're interviewing for a job. Let the company manager you're interviewing with run the show. Answer questions promptly and with brevity. Be specific. If it helps, write out a script beforehand extolling your virtues. Anticipate questions such as, "What strengths would you bring to the job?" or

"Why do you want to work at our company?" Questions such as these almost certainly will be asked.

Bad-Mouthing Former Firms, Bosses, and Coworkers

Why on earth job candidates seem compelled to bad-mouth a former boss or coworker is beyond me. Regaling your bar buddies with the tale of how you told your old boss to "take this job and shove it" is one thing; offering it up in a job interview as evidence of your worthiness for a new job is another. To paraphrase Barbra Streisand, people— especially people who hire other people—like positive attitudes.

Smoking, Drinking, or Chewing Gum

Unless you're being interviewed by R. J. Reynolds, Seagram's, or J. R. Wrigley, smoking, drinking, and chewing gum are out. Even if you are being interviewed by these or similar companies, refrain anyway. There'll be plenty of time for one or all after you get home.

Taking a "What's in It for Me" Attitude

If you're barely five minutes into a job interview and you've already asked how much vacation time you can expect, you can pretty much count yourself out of the running. The same thing goes for salary and benefits. Stick to what you can do to help the company, and the rest usually falls into place.

Forgetting to Ask for the Job

The late Thomas "Tip" O'Neill, a legendary U.S. congressman from Boston and former Speaker of the U.S. House of Representatives, loved to tell a story about his early days in politics. In his first election, he hustled to raise money, buy radio time, meet voters, and grab the right political vibes needed to win office. He won, but barely. Later he was walking down a Boston street when he met an old lady who pulled him aside and told him he didn't get her vote. Flustered, he asked why. "Because you never asked me for it, and the other guy did." Job seekers make the same mistake. They may demonstrate command of the job requirements, the right experience, and a proper attitude, but they might be beat out by a person who had the same attributes and one more—the humility to ask for the job.

Other job interview disqualifiers? Glancing at your watch, proffering a handshake only a fish would approve of, and sitting mutely through an interview session come to mind.

The best thing to do in a job interview is to relax and be yourself. Even if you don't get the job, you'll still have your integrity.

Poor First Impressions

Congratulations, you got the job. Now try to avoid the "honeymoon period" mistakes that often stop a career move in its tracks.

Nobody should tell you to change your personality on the job. But toning down personality traits that might cause you professional grief may not be a bad idea. For example, a talkative type shows up for a new job as a marketing executive at a consumer goods company. In his first meeting, when he might be taking notes, listening to his new coworkers, and generally sizing up his new workplace, the new executive barges right in and yaps up a storm. He talks down to people, telling them that his old firm "didn't do things that way." He dismisses other people's opinions, laying the groundwork for office enemies he doesn't want or need. He rolls his eyes, wrinkles his nose, and sighs heavily as others hold forth. In general, he acts like an ass.

What do you think his chances are for success at his new company? If you answered about the same chances of the Academy Awards show being moved from Hollywood to Des Moines, you get the picture.

Here's another example. A talented graphic designer snares a high-paying job at a downtown advertising agency. She starts out great but soon lapses into bad habits, such as showing up late, leaving early, and calling in sick. Another graphic designer, not as talented, started roughly at the same time. She does good work but not like the first "newbie." But she shows up early, works late, and is rarely absent from work. Soon a new job in the department opens up as creative director of the graphics division.

Who gets the job? The dependable one, that's who. Companies like continuity and order. Nothing demonstrates continuity and order like an employee who shows up at a new job on time and doesn't take sick time unless it's necessary.

Poor Workplace Traits

Once happily ensconced in a job and career, some people grow complacent. Like a married couple whose 10-year anniversary is disappearing in the rear view mirror, these people begin to take their jobs for granted and their positions in the company as untouchable.

Soon they demonstrate personal traits and characteristics that aren't exactly admirable. How can you tell? Easy. Watch for the employees who

- *Complain all the time.* Whiners can kill team morale. They're always part of the problem but rarely part of the solution.
- *Slough off.* Some people stop trying to grow and get better once they're firmly established with a company. They stop asking questions, stop taking classes, and stop moving forward. Nobody's suggesting that you eat, sleep, and breathe your job, but a little extra attention to your career can go a long way.

- *Bash coworkers.* Bashers rationalize their actions as "constructive criticism." Coworkers see it as hurtful and unnecessary. Make criticism a last resort, if you use it at all.

- *Grow undependable.* No matter how capable you are, if you are constantly showing up to work late or don't follow up on commitments, your career will suffer.

- *Refuse to get along with the boss.* Many people complain about their bosses but never consider that the relationship is really a two-way street. Make sure that your boss knows what your concerns are rather than making him guess. Also try to compliment your boss now and then. Like it or not, managing upstream is a crucial part of the working relationship.

- *Blame others.* It is always best to take responsibility for your mistakes or shortcomings and then present a solid plan of action for improving the situation.

- *Pick cliques and ostracize others.* You're judged by the company you keep, and if you hang around with people who are known as perpetual complainers, it can rub off on you. It is best to stick with the positive folks.

- *Air their dirty laundry.* Bringing personal problems into the workplace is unacceptable. Marital problems, financial difficulties, or other personal issues should be left at the door.

- *Disrespect the company.* You don't have to agree with every decision your company makes, but if you're unhappy, it's best to just find yourself another job rather than talk negatively about your employer. Disloyalty will only create a more uncomfortable work experience.

- *Grow selfish.* Employees who constantly "look out for number one" are quite annoying to both management and peers. Do you complain about your low salary? Do you consider promotions owed to you rather than something that must be earned? Do you use your maximum sick time, viewing it as extra vacation time? Your focus should be on finding ways to help your company instead of benefiting or promoting yourself. Don't be overly preoccupied with whether or not you are getting everything you deserve. This shows that you have a very narrow focus. You are much more likely to realize career advancement and personal satisfaction with a "big picture" mindset.

- *Avoid accountability.* It is refreshing when employees admit their errors and view them as opportunities to learn. After all, how much imagination does it take to make excuses? A much more admirable approach would be to own up to the fact that the mistake was yours. Then go a step further and explain your plan for both correcting and avoiding it in the future. Employees who accept responsibility demonstrate professional maturity and confidence. Your credibility will be higher if you are honest about your errors and strive to correct them.

- *Put themselves above menial tasks.* If the copier jams while you're using it, don't just walk away; fix it. No one may notice that you've fixed it, but they're sure to notice if you don't.

- *Criticize management.* Obviously, this is a no-no, even if your point of view is correct. Those who would rather be right than promoted almost always get their wish.

- *Don't work well with others.* If people don't want to be around you, your career is in trouble. Bullying, isolation, and being out of the loop in various ways all torpedo corporate careers.

Then there are the two biggest impediments to work success—*lack of ambition* and *making excuses.*

Lack of Ambition

It's said that flea-training professionals—yes, they do exist—have an interesting story to tell on this insect's peculiar behavior. The flea, it seems, has limits. Put it in a box, and the little devil will at first jump up and down like a miniature Dallas Cowboy's cheerleader at the Super Bowl. Thing is, it keeps hitting its head on the little box its trainer put it in. Ouch!

But the flea isn't stupid. Once it realizes the pain it's in, it reduces the height of its jumps. That's right—it stops hitting the top of the box when it jumps. So it reduces its jumping capacity even as it continues to jump, jump, jump. As any flea trainer will tell you—that's what a flea does. It jumps.

Okay, here's the point. When a flea trainer takes the top off a box, a flea still won't jump any higher. It's hard-wired to jump only as high as it needs to. So, it will never jump out of a box that recently held a lid.

Here's the payoff now. Like the flea, people jump only so high—high enough to survive and get by but not high enough to breathe the rarified air of career serenity.

The moral of the story. Don't be a flea—be free. And jump as high as you want.

Making Excuses

You've heard of Murphy's law, right? That anything that can go wrong will go wrong? This gem was Murphy's first law—here are the others, according to the Murphy's law site (http://www.fileoday.com/murphy/murphy-laws.html) on the World Wide Web.

1. If anything can go wrong, it will.

2. If there is a possibility of several things going wrong, the one that will cause the most damage will be the one to go wrong. Corollary: If there is a worse time for something to go wrong, it will happen then.

3. If anything just cannot go wrong, it will anyway.

4. If you perceive that there are four possible ways in which something can go wrong, and circumvent these, then a fifth way, unprepared for, will promptly develop.

5. Left to themselves, things tend to go from bad to worse.

6. If everything seems to be going well, you obviously overlooked something.

7. Nature always sides with the hidden flaw.

8. Mother nature is a bitch.

The common thread running through Murphy's law is the excuse. Career professionals who make excuses often find themselves wondering why they're not getting ahead in the workplace and in their careers.

It's easy to see why. Instead of rolling up your sleeves and finding new ways to look at a problem, it's much easier to say, "Forget it," that there is no other way to solve the problem and that you've wasted enough time on it. It is worth remembering that people who start companies—entrepreneurs and such—are not excuse makers and have no patience with people who are. So chances are that the person running your company is such an entrepreneur and surely will pass you over when promotions roll around in favor of someone who didn't make excuses and found innovative ways to solve challenging problems. There's nothing worse in an entrepreneur's mind than an employee who settles for excuses or for rationalization.

Maybe it's their fault, and maybe it's not. Maybe they're not getting enough sleep, eating right, exercising, or getting their personal act together in general. Often these are the same people who cruise the Web all day, take personal phone calls as a birthright, and treat the office supply room as their own personal Staples.

But if you recognize any of these traits in yourself, rest assured that your employers do, too.

Management Blunders to Avoid

Getting promoted to management is a big deal. It is not so big, however, that it should change the workplace ways that have worked so well for you in the past.

But a taste of power can bedevil the most honorable professionals. Some handle it well, and others don't. The ones who don't often make the following mistakes:

Failing to Communicate

A well-informed group of employees is one of the most important ingredients of a healthy, upbeat workplace. But don't just communicate the big picture. The seemingly little things—the broken coffee pot, slight changes to the work schedule, the new format of payroll checks—are often just as important to employees. By talking about the little things, you'll prevent gossip and rumors and foster a sense of ownership.

Taking Too Much Responsibility

This is a common problem among inexperienced managers. By delegating liberally, you not only keep your own desk clear, you also give employees the opportunity to solve problems on their own and grow toward their own potential.

Personalizing Issues

Sure, you're angry when an employee is late three days in a row or when an important task isn't completed on time. But remember, when you turn a work-related issue into a personal one, you can easily spark personal animosity on the part of the people around you. Always maintain professional objectivity and decorum, whatever the issue and no matter how upset you might feel inside.

Holding Your Cards Too Long

Managers often notice problems in the workplace but wait too long to act on them. Sometimes they're preoccupied, sometimes it's a personality issue, and sometimes they just don't want to rock the boat. All too often managers wait until an annual review or, worse, a layoff notice to tell the employee that there's a problem. This not only stuns the unfortunate employee, it also lowers morale among other workers who might wonder if they're on some kind of hit list, too.

Being an Ingrate

One of the most common complaints of employees is that management doesn't positively recognize their contributions to the company. Some managers might think that they are too busy to say "Thank you" or that a paycheck is thanks enough. They're missing the point. Saying "Thanks" is a wonderful way to boost morale at no cost to the budget. Besides, it's the polite thing to do.

Failing to Motivate

It's easy to assume that the weekly paycheck alone motivates employees. Experienced managers, however, know that this isn't true. Other motivators—benefits packages, opportunities for personal and professional growth, friendships on the job, and the opportunity to learn—can all be vital to employees. The wise manager discovers what triggers the interest of each employee and responds accordingly.

Becoming a "One Note" Manager

You might think that managers should treat every employee identically. This is only fair, right? Wrong. No two employees possess the same skills, temperament, or experience, and no two employees need exactly the same kind of supervision. Some employees need a fixed routine. Others need the opportunity to demonstrate creativity. Some need an opportunity for highly structured relationships with a supervisor. Others need constant feedback. Figure out what each employee needs to do the job effectively—and treat each employee accordingly.

Forgeting That Loyalty Is a Two-Way Street

Managers usually expect employees to show loyalty to them, but often they forget that loyalty is a two-way street. You can demonstrate loyalty by making affirming comments to employees, wishing them well on special occasions, paying attention to their personal needs, and using their mistakes as mutual learning opportunities.

Failing to Consider All Employees as Equal Partners

Trust is established when even the newest rookie, a part-timer, or the lowest paid employee feels important and part of the team. This begins with management not being aloof, as well as getting out and meeting the troops. This should be followed by leaders seeking opinions and ideas (and giving credit for them), knowing the names of employees and their families, and treating one and all with genuine respect.

Contradicting Yourself

Nothing confuses people faster than inconsistency. And if confusion due to contradiction is the only constant, trust is sure to fall victim.

Getting Selfish

A manager who is out only for himself, especially in a team environment, quickly loses the respect and trust of others.

Closing the Lines of Communication

When the communication channels shut down—both top-down and bottom-up—rumors start, and misinformation is believed to be real. Then come denials. True information is often too late or is never offered. Then trust falls apart.

Neglecting to Tell the Truth

Nobody likes a liar. Once you lie to an employee, it's almost impossible to get her trust back.

Being Dictatorial

Managers who use such phrases as "My way or the highway" or "I know what's best" are managers who don't listen to their employees. Not only does this behavior squander a valuable source of information, it also sends a message that employees don't matter.

REALITY CHECK: LOOSE LIPS SINK CAREER SHIPS

Kathy Donaldson was a victim of circumstance—but she survived to tell the tale.

Donaldson, a longtime nurse practitioner in a major university hospital, saw firsthand how rumors and gossip can poison a workplace and kill careers.

"I'd been sick with the flu, which turned into pneumonia, and I wound up being out of work for a while," she recalls. "I lived in a double-decker townhouse, and a coworker's husband drove by one Monday morning on the way to work and saw a stack of empty beer cases and liquor bottles from my downstairs neighbor, who'd had a big party the previous Saturday night. Putting two and two together—and getting five—the husband mentioned to my coworker (a notorious gossip) that he'd seen empty liquor bottles outside my house, which he thought was pretty strange from someone who was supposed to be sick.

"The next day I get a call from my boss saying that people were talking about my 'problem.' It seemed my coworker had blabbed to one and all that I wasn't legitimately sick, but was carrying on like a crazed drunk and was ruining my health.

"My boss knew I was a teetotaler and told her to stop immediately. When she didn't—and I came back to work to square things up—I had her written up. It seems that she'd passed on rumors and gossip before, and the next thing I knew, she wasn't working there anymore. They'd let her go for spreading false information about her coworkers."

Donaldson said she was sorry to see her coworker go, but understood why. "Management felt like they couldn't trust a person like that," she explains. "In a hospital, where confidentiality is critical, you can't afford to have a loose cannon around. People, especially patients and their families, could really get hurt by hearing false information. So she had to go."

5

Help Me Now, I'm Falling:
Anticipating—and Surviving—
a Layoff

There undoubtedly will be times in your career when you're going to face more adversity than you may think you can handle. Maybe you feel like you've already faced such a challenge. It could be a boss with the warmth of Count Dracula or a coworker with a vast collection of sharp kitchen cutlery on hand to stab you and your associates in the back. Or you could walk back to your desk one day and find an e-mail from human resources telling you that your job has been eliminated.

The important point to remember when dealing with adverse times, especially when layoffs are in the air, is that it matters less what happens to you than how you handle yourself.

Take Apple Computer founder and chief executive officer Steve Jobs. In 1983, Jobs was the largest stockholder in Apple Computer, at a time when the company stock was selling for more than $60 per share. Jobs, who always had a mystical bent about him, felt the sting of the stock market when a year later his company's stock price had plummeted. His loss was over $250 million. Asked what it was like to lose that sum of money, Jobs was nonplussed. "It's very character building," he said.

Now that's resilience. But there's another side to adversity that you should know about—the notion that adversity may close one door and open another.

There's an old proverb about facing adversity that's also worth knowing. Two acorns taken from the same oak tree and identical in size and shape are planted, one in a dense forest and one on a hill overlooking a massive plain. Before long, the small oak tree standing alone on the hill is besieged by the elements. Its roots reach out in every direction, clutching the rocks and piercing deep into the earth. Every root is meant to stabilize the growing giant, as if in anticipation of rough storms and winds to come. When the gales do come, they find that the burgeoning oak, anchored now by a firm network of roots, is more than a match for the raging elements. Now the acorn planted deep in the woods merely shoots up a slender sapling. Shielded by taller neighbors, the small tree feels no urgency to spread its roots far and wide for support.

The lesson? We grow from adversity.

TOUGH TIMES AHEAD? HERE'S WHAT TO DO

Resiliency, opportunism, and preparedness are all worthy attitudes to take when times are tough, the economy's going into the tank, and you hear the first whispers that your company is going to begin laying off workers. Unfortunately, millions of Americans found such rumors to be true in 2000 and 2001 as the dot-com demise combined with a falling stock market and the terrorist attacks on New York City and Washington, D.C., to produce a sour business climate where pink slips rained from the sky.

In times like these, morale is going to suffer, and anxiety can carry the day. The best way to stay afloat in uncertain economic times and ride out a wave of layoffs at your company is to be ready and to take certain steps that remind management of your value and importance to the company. If the ax falls anyway, then it's best to be prepared for that, too, with a blueprint to rebound from a layoff and come back stronger than ever. (Remember, a layoff doesn't ruin a career. In fact, it might create opportunities that you never knew existed.)

Also remember that this isn't your father's career either. Today's corporate climate doesn't guarantee anyone a job for life. Given the fact that you really can't count on your loyalty to your company (actually the only loyalty you should have is to your career), you need to be creative to get ahead in the good times and survive the bad ones. This means working smart and having a plan you can turn to when the job picture dims. People who are in charge of their own careers are constantly developing and marketing themselves. They're continually letting people know what they bring to the table. This attitude can land you a new, better job—or spare you when colleagues are getting the ax.

In addition, management looks for certain types of employees who are indispensable and certain types of employees who are expendable when scouting for layoff candidates. Knowing what those characteristics and personality traits are is a big advantage for an employee, especially since most of their coworkers have no idea what steps they might take to keep their positions when the pink slips hit the fan.

The first trick is to recognize when layoffs are barreling down the pipeline. Let's take a look at keys that can tell you a company is ready to begin layoffs and what you can do to survive.

Anticipating a Layoff

You'd never know it from talking to your boss, but companies that are about to embark on a job-cutting campaign leave more clues around the workplace than the most inept burglar.

Knowing what those clues are and using them to your advantage can be the difference between losing a job or keeping one. Even if you do lose your job, being prepared for it can make all the difference in the world.

Consider the bank customer service representative who heard rumors of an impending layoff at her firm. Immediately she began researching possible business ideas in her spare time. Remanufacturing printer toner cartridges seemed to have potential, so the bank staffer began operating a new business out of her basement. When the layoff came, she was able to hit the ground running, and her cartridge business began to grow. Within three years, her little startup had become one of the 100 largest printer cartridge remanufacturers in the country in an industry of over 9000 competitors.

Therefore, if you begin to suspect that something's amiss at your company and that job cuts are headed down the pike, here are some clues to look for so that you too can plan ahead.

You Lose Key Privileges

If you travel a lot and have your itinerary reduced or hear that your company cell phone is being taken away, you probably will be told that the moves are based on cost cutting and have no reflection on your job security. Individually, this may be true. But if both happen in the same month (or worse, the same week), this is a big red flag.

You're Singled Out

Let's say that every year a key client gives everyone in your department a fruit basket or gift certificate for the holidays. If the gifts arrived and you don't get one, then it's possible that your biggest client already knows that job cuts are on the way and that your job is among them.

Underlings Share Your Time in Big Meetings

In the first wave of a layoff, many companies like to replace more experienced, and more expensive, employees with cheaper and younger workers. This is so because the move has the most impact on the bottom line—a bouquet for Wall Street, if you will. So if you see subordinates beginning to creep more and more into meetings formerly limited to VIPs, this could be a sign that layoffs are imminent and that younger workers are being groomed to take older workers' positions.

You're Assigned to a Corporate Charity

On the list of critical business issues, running the corporate charity ranks down there between who pays for the beer after the weekly softball game and what brand of staplers the company should use. So if you're given the task of running the big boss's favorite charity, try not to take it as a compliment. First, charity work is time-consuming, so you won't have much time for your other work. Second, it may be a sign that your company doesn't know what to do with you and is buying time before laying you off.

Know the Lingo

When companies walk around using such language as "We're going to refocus on our core business" or "We're going to reexamine our business efficiencies," run, don't walk, to the nearest computer and start firing off copies of your résumé. Such phrases are code words for imminent layoffs.

You're Coworkers Are Bored

A decreased workload may be one of the top telltale signs that a layoff is in the works. If you see the engineering department gathering around the water cooler for long stretches of time or the marketing department playing Doom on their computers, this is a good sign that workloads are down and cuts are on the way.

You're Isolated

This is kind of like the charity issue. If you find yourself spending too much time on your own or, worse, that employees seem to be shunning you, something is amiss. People may have heard something, or maybe management doesn't want to assign you to the big new project because your replacement is already being interviewed. This is painful to acknowledge but good to know. On another note, if your isolation is self-imposed, this is a problem, too. Hiding in your cubicle can mean all the hard work you've done could go unnoticed if you don't let coworkers and bosses know what you have accomplished.

A Rise in Security Staffing

Another telltale sign that job cuts are imminent is when a company beefs up its security detail. Companies will do this to ensure that laid-off workers exit the premises without taking a swing at the chief executive officer (CEO) or emptying their wastebaskets on the human resources director's head. If you notice two or three Barney Fife types strolling about with badges and uniforms with snappy security company logos on their shirts and you haven't seen them before, something is up.

Managers Install Privacy Screens on Their Computers

One former dot-commer mentioned this one to me. She was assigned to hand out new meeting schedules to managers at her company, a job she'd done in the past. Walking from office to office, she noticed that all the computer screens in the managers' offices were covered with special privacy shields so that nobody could see what each manager was working on. It turns out that management was working on a reduced head count. Layoffs began the following week.

The Kinds of Employees Management Lays Off

Don't kid yourself. Management will make it as easy as possible on itself when forced to choose layoff candidates. Frequently managers are given a head-count target by human resources but are left to their own judgment as to which employees to let go. A good rereading of Chapter 4 should give you a solid idea of what character traits managers look for in employees they keep and employees they let go during a layoff. Workers who are frequently absent or late, those who do sloppy work, and gossips and shirkers are at the top of the list of likely candidates to pack their bags. Conversely, companies often keep workers with good attendance records, solid communication skills, and multiple workplace strengths when push comes to shove.

Whatever you do, don't give management a reason to let you go. Frequently, layoff lists come down to personality quirks and politics as often as they do to experience and salaries. Here are a few workplace traits management will penalize at layoff time:

Copping a Negative Attitude

Complaining to coworkers about an aspect of your job is not a good idea. Complaining about coworkers is even worse (and complaining about a manager may be suicide).

Too Cool for School

From the "It takes one to know one" category, management doesn't like prima donnas (maybe because they remind them of themselves). Therefore, don't be above menial tasks. If the copier jams while you're using it, don't just walk away; fix it. If you empty the coffee pot, refill it. Sure, they seem like small things, but word will get around that you're a team player, and that can give you the edge come layoff time

Helping Thyself

If you constantly use company resources for personal matters, this will reflect poorly on you when job-cut decisions are being made. Many companies monitor their employees' use of computers. Using company e-mail to send personal messages, shopping on the Internet, and making too many personal phone calls are considered theft by many employers. And if you have a reputation as someone who revels in the personal phone call, this won't help you either.

Job Hopping

This may not seem fair in the information age, where employees can land new jobs on the Internet in days (sometimes hours). But if given a choice, management may opt to keep the person with the stable job track record over the one who's working on her fourth job in 14 months.

Curse Your Independence

Again, this may not reflect on your job capabilities, but often the first people cut in a layoff are the hoards of independent contractors and freelancers the company accumulated during the boom times.

Therefore, if the rumors are flying and you're among the few, the proud, and the chosen of the contracting elite, prepare for a direct hit in the coming weeks.

The One-Hit Wonder

Despite plenty of information to the contrary, management isn't stupid. Give the option of keeping a computer programmer who can pound out code in five different computing languages and can troubleshoot hard-drive problems on the side or keeping a programmer who can only write programs in one code, management will choose the former over the latter almost every time. The only exceptions I can think of are if the one-hit wonder is related to the boss or if he has incriminating pictures of the boss. Other than this, management will go with the multitalented employee every time.

Parents Versus Singletons

There's no telling if a given company makes distinctions about keeping working parents over single workers, or vice versa. In many cases, companies love the fact that singletons usually can work those extra hours at night, when most parents are home tucking their little moppets into bed. On the other hand, companies like to have a family-friendly image. They may keep the parents over the singles, especially given the fact that most parents are older and theoretically possess more experience and value to the company in a bare-bones economic period when the company needs employees with those attributes. Of course, since singles are younger and less experienced, they're paid less, too. This could be a deciding factor in their favor if a company is really trying to cut the budget to the bone. Use your best judgment here. If your company seems to reward people who work late and can be called out of bed on Christmas Eve for an emergency, then being single is probably an advantage. But if your company has an onsite day-care center, flex-hours, and other family-friendly perks, being a parent isn't a problem. A tip: If your CEO is a parent, chances are that he will take other parents' situations into consideration when deliberating job cuts. If your head honcho is single, then parental considerations aren't as big an issue when deciding who stays and who goes.

HOW TO REDUCE YOUR CHANCES OF BEING LAID OFF

While negative workplace characteristics may stand out more when management is hunting for pink-slip candidates, it's the foolish CEO who doesn't order his managers to accentuate the positive, too. They usually keep the following attributes in mind when tallying the pros and cons of layoff candidates.

Reliability

You show up on time and stay late. You also don't make a fuss when handed tough projects.

Organization

You are a worker who keeps clean desks and can self-promote yourself by keeping a monthly log of your achievements and what obstacles you overcame to achieve those results.

Versatility

You're eager to learn new skills and fill in on jobs unrelated to yours. You train yourself to become more valuable by taking classes and attending seminars.

Risk Taking

Management rewards workers who offer to take on the difficult project that no one else wants and find solutions.

Loyalty

This may be the attribute a CEO (especially if the CEO founded the company) values most. If you've been with the company for years, chances are that this will work in your favor when layoff decisions are made. Loyalty means a lot to managers who are never really sure who they can depend on. And nothing spells loyalty like time on the job.

Profit Center Producers

Management hates to lay off people who contribute directly to the bottom line. Top salespeople, for instance, are usually untouchable in pink-slip situations. So are employees who can prove that they bring projects in on time and under budget. Computer specialists are also treated with kid gloves by management. It's hard to run a company when the information technology director who purchased and installed your most recent computing platform is out on the street.

Team Attitude

Didn't you just hate those kids in high school who ran around extolling the values of school spirit? Me, too. The bad news is that they've grown up to become the cheerleaders of your workplace. And guess what? Management loves them. In fact, management will always reward workers who can make others feel good and maintain morale.

SO YOU'VE BEEN LAID OFF—WHAT NOW?

Like the book says, bad things can happen to good people—and often do. Ask any Boston Red Sox fan or anybody who has been forced to accompany a loved one to a Marilyn Manson concert.

So it goes with a corporate layoff when all of your accomplishments and all your achievements are overlooked by cold-hearted managers obsessed with an artificially imposed head-count reduction that serves Wall Street but rarely Main Street.

But if you prepare in advance for a layoff, you'll be ready should the inevitable happen. Of course you'll be disappointed. Of course you'll miss your old friends and the routine of your old job. And of course you'll worry about your finances. Remember, though, that a layoff isn't the end of the world—often it's the start of a new one. A personal note: I was laid off from my last corporate job in 1995. Tired of answering to people but with a brand-new baby daughter on hand, I decided to damn the torpedoes and strike out on my own as a freelance writer. It's a decision that has worked out well career-wise over the years but one that I never would have made if I hadn't become a dues-paying member of head count nation. A bonus: I got to see my daughter take her first steps, was there when she fell off her tricycle, and put her on her first bus to kindergarten—a process I've repeated twice now with her two younger brothers. I've often thought of sending my last boss a box of candy or a bottle of wine in gratitude for giving me the chance to watch my kids grow up, let alone the other career stuff. But then I think better of it and opt to keep the wine for my wife and me and the candy for the kids.

So take it from someone who's been there. Sure, being downsized can leave you feeling discouraged, disillusioned, and defeated. After a while, though, such behavior is self-defeating and ultimately a waste of time. I'm not saying that you can't grieve for a little while or feel sorry for yourself for a day or two. Be my guest. It's only human to want to climb under the covers with a box of double-stuffed Oreos or hit the local watering hole for a few well-deserved belts. But get that stuff over with quickly, and get on with the pressing business of moving your career forward. Here are some tips that will allow you to do just that.

Don't Take It Personally

No matter how awful you feel, downsizing is a business decision that has nothing to do with you. It has everything to do with the company's bottom line. Also try to remember that the decision was not about your skills, ability to do the job, or personal worth. Remember this too— you are not alone. By some estimates, more than 10 million Americans have been downsized.

Assess the Situation

The reason why I spent so much time talking about knowing that a layoff is coming and preparing for it is that they can give you the opportunity to absorb the blow and give you more time to develop a blueprint for what happens next. They also give you the chance to bone up on your company's severance package or mull over the idea of going back to school or launching your own home-based business. The important thing is to leave all options open and give yourself some time to weigh the pros and cons of each one. The last thing you want to do after losing your job is to make a snap judgment that you might regret later. Sure, you'll be tempted to take the next available job offer. But is it right for you?

The interval immediately after losing your job is a great time to learn all you can about yourself. Identify your strengths, achievements, interests, and values, and write them down. Not only will this information help you set new goals, but it will also help you see where you best fit in. Self-examination can help you prepare for job interviews and regain your confidence.

Conduct Your Own Due Diligence Campaign

When you get the bad news, one of the first things you should do is to pull out the employee handbook and all your benefits literature and read them cover to cover. I know, this is tedious work. Doing so, however, can make a big difference in the first weeks and months following a layoff. You want to be sure that you know exactly what you are entitled to be paid and what, if any, financial benefits, such as unused vacation pay or stock option cashouts, you're entitled to. Health care benefits will be crucial, too. Normally COBRA benefits run out after 60 days, at which time the financial obligation for your health plan reverts from your company to you. Also get yourself an agreement from someone in the company to be your reference later on. Most companies will just give out your name and dates of employment.

Change Can Be Positive

Perhaps you saw the writing on the wall at your company. Financial reports were not looking good, your department was not getting much support, or your project got canceled. In such cases, layoffs can lead to positive change. Your old position might have been heading toward a dead end, especially in light of the volatile economic situation. Layoffs can be springboards to a fresh start.

What Do I Want in My Next Job—Or Do I Even Want a Next Job?

Whether you anticipate a layoff in your near future or have already received your pink slip, take this time as an opportunity to analyze what you really want to do next. Ask yourself what you really enjoy doing. Who among us hasn't had a father or mother who once told us, "Do what you love, and the money will follow." This is a quaint phrase that's a little too cute for me, but it does make a lot of sense. After all, life is short—why spend it doing something you are not passionate about? This is what I mean when I say that layoffs also bring opportunity. They provide some time to sit back and reflect and figure out what career or vocation will bring out the passion in you. For me, it was writing. For someone else, it might be opening a diner or working at a bookstore. I know what you're thinking. "I've got a mortgage and kids to feed. And this clown is raving about passion and diners and bookstores?" But if you really love what you're doing, money won't matter as much. You'll be happier and more productive and a better husband/wife/friend/partner, etc. Besides, the money issue usually works itself out when you're doing something you love.

Ask for Help

If you lose your job, the worst thing you can do is to go it alone. You have friends, you have family, and you have coworkers—many of whom have lost their jobs, too. Talk to them and hang out with them. Break out your Rolodex and start e-mailing career contacts you've made. See if they know of any job openings. Check with your former employer and see if the firm offers any outplacement assistance. Don't be too proud to ask for help. People won't mind and will, by and large, go to bat for you. After all, they may need your help someday.

Polish Your Résumé

Keep your résumé updated with fresh references. Add new accomplishments every six months. Employers are interested most in career achievements, demonstrated skills, education, and stability, so place the most interesting and compelling facts at the beginning of your résumé. List measurable accomplishments in order of relevance. Include specific key words and phrases, and use numbers; for example, "Increased U.S. sales of broadband Internet services by 50 percent in six months."

Keep your résumé to one page, ideally. A hiring manager once told me that she throws away résumés that are longer than one page. "If you can't sum up your career on one sheet of paper, then chances are you can't handle working for me either." Translated: If you waste my time now, you'll waste my time later. Ouch! This is tough love but good advice.

Get Web Savvy

Post your résumé, and search job databases. The Internet is a vital component to a job search. Job seekers can post résumés online at various career Web sites or other local Web sites. This is a quick and easy way to let prospective employers know that you're available. Also search online databases for available jobs of interest to you. Monster.com, CareerCity.com, Resumes.com, and FlipDog.com are among the best Web sites for job seekers.

Leave with Class

Let's face it. Many companies that are strapped for cash have to get rid of perfectly smart and great employees they just don't need or can't afford anymore. You just can't take it personally. In fact, it's better to take it professionally.

Yet people—understandably ticked off about being let go—can react hysterically, even aggressively, to such an event. Reports from the dot-com implosion of 2000 and 2001 included stories of laid-off "techies" who overturned desks, stole computers, wrote obscenities on walls, and so forth.

If you lose your job, why be graceless when you can be graceful about it? One woman who worked at a graphic design firm found out that she was going to be laid off months in advance. Instead of wailing and gnashing her teeth and wishing a plague of locusts on her boss, she set about finishing her last few projects with great care and detail. Coyly, she let her company's clients know that she was earmarked for dismissal, but she cheerfully reminded them that her work would remain top-notch and that their projects would be completed on time. Instead of being bitter (like most of her coworkers), she believed that by finishing her projects during the final months and remaining friendly with her company and its customers, she would cushion the blow of a layoff. Sure enough, she got an offer from a client to come work for her at a better salary. In short, this worker decided not simply to avoid burning old bridges but to build new ones. One other point on leaving a company with dignity: Once you hit the ranks of the unemployed, contacts are going to be like gold. If you remain on good terms with your old company, this will expand the pool of possible networking contacts you'll need for your next career move, be it starting a business or finding a new job. In addition, you may be able to freelance for your old company or for old clients while you plan your future. Many companies that do not have the ability to pay a full salary may be able to pay for some contracting work here and there. While you're looking for a job—or even taking an extended vacation—some of that extra freelancing cash from your former company could come in handy.

Plan Ahead to Get All the Information You Need

Back in the prehistoric days of 1975, when slide rule–wielding engineers walked the earth, laid-off employees could at least console themselves with the fact that they received the news face to face from their bosses. At least then you could hear a manager express his regret and thank you for your contribution. He might even have offered severance pay if you'd been employed there for a while. You'd be allowed enough time to clear your desk and say goodbye to your coworkers; there'd be a feeling of respectful regret and dignity. Now chances are you'll get the bad news via e-mail from a faceless drone in human resources who doesn't know you, hasn't worked with you, and has no idea what contributions you've made to the company. At certain companies, some of the technology tools are more nefarious. For the unprepared, log-ons may cease to work, mobile phones may go dead, and lifeless security key cards can lead to noses smashing against glass doors. Welcome to the spam-style layoff.

The information age brings other issues to the table after a layoff as well. For instance, that e-mail notice telling you that you're history also may include a line or two about evacuating the premises immediately and notifying you that your computer password is no longer active. The last one hurts because you're probably going to want your old computer files for your next career step.

If you work for a company that doesn't use technology in a cowardly manner to give you the bad news, you might have 30 days to access your e-mail. The company might even offer the use of an outplacement service that offers use of phones, faxes, and computers or provides access from your personal laptop or home computer. A really nice company will let you keep the laptop it gave you.

Still, some companies worry that downsized workers will take information with them that legally belongs to the company. Others fear that laid-off workers will resort to electronic sabotage. This is why many require all downsized workers to return equipment before they leave, and this is why you should download key career information regularly to your home computer or laptop. Such information may include

- Annual reviews
- Key industry contacts
- A résumé and cover letter
- E-mail addresses
- An online calendar
- Bookmarked Web sites
- Personal notes and accomplishments (Keep an online journal of projects you've finished or awards you've won, and have it ready to go, in addition to an updated résumé.)

Action Items When You've Lost a Job

- Keep getting up in the morning. You will find another job. Remember, you have skills!
- Contact your state unemployment office immediately to get the typical waiting period out of the way for your unemployment checks.

- Update and polish your résumé.

- Start searching for a new job right away.

- Submit your updated résumé to several job sites to let employers come to you.

- Apply to receive job notification by e-mail at job sites that offer it to let the jobs come to you, too.

- Contact your references to let them know that you're back in the job market and counting on them.

- Ask your ex-boss to write a recommendation letter that also explains why the job loss wasn't your fault.

- Practice interviewing while you have the time and to keep your confidence level up.

- Attend outplacement seminars if offered.

- Consider temping until you find a permanent job. Some of the best jobs start as a temporary or part-time position.

- Keep sleep patterns consistent. Always get good rest and go to bed and get up the same time every day, even on weekends.

- Volunteer. Stay a part of the community while giving yourself the gift of fulfillment and others the gift of your time and experience.

- Learn how to use a computer. Take a class or ask someone to show you the basics—or if you already know the basics, learn a new program that will help improve your chances of getting a good job.

- Contact your automobile insurance agency. You may be eligible for reduced rates because you will no longer be traveling to and from work every day. Ask about recreational-use-only rates.

- Keep track of receipts for all job search–related expenses. Many are tax deductible, such as, gas, tolls, paper for résumés, etc.
- Prepare for a job search or interview the night before. Have your clothes ready, watch the weather report and dress accordingly, do personal grooming, go to bed early, put gas in the car or get tokens or change for public transportation, plan breakfast, and set your alarm clock to give yourself plenty of time to prepare in a nonrushed, stress-free manner.

These tips will help you through this transitional time in your life:

- Take care of your body. Eat well. Exercise. Avoid drugs and alcohol.
- Review your finances. Figure out a budget for the next six months. (Most people find work within 90 days.)
- Cut costs by not using credit cards, eating in restaurants, or shopping in malls.
- Check with the utility company and credit card agencies about a reduced payment plan.

REALITY CHECK: READING—AND RESPONDING TO—RED FLAGS

Some signs that a company is going downhill fast are obvious. A plummeting stock price, hoards of disappearing customers, or abrupt changes in senior management can give things away.

But knowing the subtler signs of a company in distress helped Brian Bullard jump ship in advance of its sinking and enabled him to hook up with a healthier company with a rosy future.

What were those signs? "They were really subtle," said the 35-year-old software engineer (nicknamed "Bull" by his friends). "I noticed that management had stopped paying for meals for people who worked through dinner, which was a staple ever since I got to the firm. My friends said it was a simple cost-cutting measure, but I wasn't sure.

"Then we got word that the conference room was off limits for the next week or so. The board of directors would be coming in for a 'strategy session' and would need the space. That sounded fishy to me."

Finally, Bullard was friendly with the building's security director. "One day he joked to me that my firm must be swimming in money because he'd had a request from my bosses to hire three or four more security people. That told me something big was coming up. I'd been courted by another software firm off and on for months, and I called them right away asking if they were still interested. They were—and the day I received my formal job offer, my current company announced they were cutting staff by 50 percent. That's what the board of directors had determined in their meeting, and that's why they felt they needed extra security help to make sure nobody stole a computer or something.

"It was funny. The week before my coworkers were calling me suspicious. A week later they were asking me if my new firm was hiring. Go figure."

6

10,000 Maniacs Was a Rock 'n' Roll Band—Not Your Workplace

There's no getting around it. There are some coworkers you're going to like and some you'll even grow to love. Then there are the coworkers you'd swear were spawned in the ninth circle of hell. You know, the steamrollers, mother superiors, buck passers, and other cubicle wildlife.

This chapter is about them.

Consider the monks who lived in the monastery on Mount Serat in Spain centuries ago. One of the fundamental requirements of this religious order was that the young men must maintain silence. Opportunities to speak were scheduled once every two years, at which time the monks were allowed to speak only two words. One young initiate in this religious order, who had completed his first two years of training, was invited by his superior to make his first two-word presentation. "Food terrible," he said. Two years later, the invitation was extended once again. The young man used this forum to exclaim, "Bed lumpy." Arriving at his superior's office two years later, he proclaimed, "I quit." The superior looked at this young monk and said, "You know, it doesn't surprise me a bit. All you've done since you arrived is complain, complain, complain."

Exaggerated? Maybe. But you're not going to get far in your career if you're always complaining and locking horns with people. It's time-consuming and energy-draining, and there's very little to gain from it even if you emerge from an intraoffice squabble victorious. Squabbles between coworkers may not appear all that debilitating. They may even prove entertaining to some of your more easily entertained coworkers. The truth is that bouts of temperament can have disastrous consequences in the workplace. Personality clashes often distract from work routines, undermine morale, jeopardize teamwork, threaten productivity, and sometimes erupt into dangerous and violent confrontations.

By and large, you don't want to get in anyone's face or make enemies, although you probably will do both at some point in your career. There is, however, an advantage in being able to identify toxic coworkers and in developing a blueprint for manipulating them rather than the other way around. In fact, learning how to deal with people is one of the top issues companies look at when promoting employees. John Rockefeller once said that he would pay more for the ability to deal with people than for any other ability under the sun.

Rockefeller had a point. A Carnegie Foundation report once stated that only 15 percent of a person's career success is attributable to such things as intelligence and experience, and 85 percent is human relations.

Another Carnegie (this one, Dale) once said that you can make more friends in two months by being interested in them than you can in two years by trying to get them interested in you. This is a great lesson to learn not just in the workplace but also in our everyday lives. However, since this book is about careers, let's focus on how to leverage the fine art of human relations to deal with that lowest of human life forms—the office troublemaker.

THE ART OF MAKING NICE

The key thing to keep in mind when dealing with difficult coworkers is that they foster negativity in the workplace. Sustained negativity is a career stopper that should, in a perfect world, be avoided like the plague. Negativity has a habit of sticking to people, good and bad, like barnacles to the hull of a boat. Soon you find that it's tough to scrape it off, and if you're not careful, it can drag you under. And this is what difficult coworkers want—for you to be as miserable as they are.

Unfortunately, it's almost impossible to avoid problem coworkers or ornery bosses (the subject of Chapter 7). In the day-to-day workings of industry, there's always going to be a fair share of whiners, tyrants, complainers, malcontents, back stabbers, and other cubicle wildlife that seemingly exist to make your life miserable. The trick is first to identify them and then to deal with them so that you come away with the answers you need to finish your project and keep your dignity intact without getting any of that nasty negativity stuff on yourself.

Dealing with nasty employees is particularly tough if you've already ascended to a supervisory or management position. According to a survey from Accountemps, a temporary help and job placement firm, management personnel now spend an average of 18 percent of their time dealing with personality clashes among employees. A similar survey in 1986 pegged the time spent refereeing intraoffice squabbles at about 10 percent.

Workplace sociologists say that the increase in workplace personality clashes stems from today's increased competition, rapid business pace, frequent restructuring, and multiple mergers. The tensions associated with downsizing often cause emotions to run close to the surface.

When workers are constantly pressured to produce more, faster, and with fewer resources, anger and frustration are natural by-products. Likewise, job uncertainty produces fear, insecurity, and anxiety. Whenever these ingredients exist in the workplace, the result is a combustible mixture that can blow up at any time. Consequently, it should come as no surprise that a greater number of workers have short fuses, are quick to anger, and come to work more ready to fight than ever before. It would be more surprising if they didn't.

With today's volatile work environment, it doesn't take much to set off an argument. Some of the specific causes that frequently trigger workplace clashes include

- Misunderstandings based on age, race, or cultural differences
- Competition that has gotten out of control
- Intolerance, prejudice, discrimination, or bigotry
- Perceived inequities
- Misunderstandings, rumors, or falsehoods about an individual or group
- Long-standing grudges (old wounds)
- Misplaced loyalties
- Fear of job loss or being bypassed for a promotion

- Sexual tensions or harassment
- Perceived threats to security, power, or status
- Workplace romances gone awry and false pride
- Comparisons of performance ratings or bonuses
- Blaming others for mistakes or mishaps (finger-pointing)
- Alcohol- or drug-induced irrational behaviors

The Rules of Engagement

Generally we think of fights as unpleasant confrontations between two or more people in which tempers flare, voices are raised, and angry insults are exchanged. Fights need not be this way. They are normal and necessary in most relationships, but dirty, unfair fights only result in bitterness, distrust, and the desire for revenge.

Clean, fair fights, on the other hand, are confrontations in which disagreements and grievances are dealt with according to a specific set of rules. At the end of a fair fight, most people feel refreshed and relieved because a sensitive issue has been settled in a constructive way.

The following rules must be observed when conducting a clean, fair fight:

- *No hitting below the belt*—purposely calling attention to known weaknesses or sensitive areas.
- *No false agreements*—pretending to go along or to agree when you don't.
- *No character analysis or psychoanalyzing*—telling people what they are thinking or feeling or why they acted as they did.
- *No stereotyping*—labeling or name-calling.
- *No gunny sacking*—saving up minor grievances and dumping them all at once rather than dealing with them one at a time as they occur.

Continued

- *No playing archaeologist*—digging up past happenings.
- *No generalizations*—using statements such as "You always . . ." or "You never . . ." to describe a person's behavior.
- *Stick to the issue*—dealing with only one issue at a time.
- *No bomb dropping*—overreacting to a situation and making idle threats or giving an ultimatum.
- *Avoid round-robin fights*—continuing with repetitive, stale arguments where no progress is being made toward conflict resolution.

The purpose of arguments and conflict is to resolve difficulties or solve problems, not to assign blame or to find fault. Do not keep score. Do not lecture. Differentiate between behavior and being. Treat everyone with regard and respect. Do not judge the perceptions and feelings of others. Accept differences. And don't forget the best part of all fights—making up afterwards. Making up is essential to complete resolution.

SHOULD YOU INTERVENE?

The variables of workplace politics surely will work to place you in the middle of a workplace free-for-all sooner rather than later, either as a direct participant or as a manager or supervisor.

You'll have to quickly identify the seriousness of the episode. If it's simply a noted office drama king/queen spouting off, chances are that things will blow over quickly. However, if someone truly becomes unhinged and begins making threats against you or another coworker, immediately go to your supervisor or company security chief. If neither is available, call 911. There have been too many instances of workplace violence in the last few years to take any chances.

Certainly those instances are the rare exception and not the rule. Probably the best advice for rank-and-file employees faced with a situation where tempers are heated and the fur starts to fly is not to take sides. When this happens, the only sure result is that you'll make at least one long-term enemy. Better to stay out of it and report anything serious, such as a threat or string of obscenities, to your manager and let him or her deal with it. Whenever you do, however, you make at least one serious enemy.

Also understand that, most of the time, office combatants are repeat offenders with hidden agendas that have little to do with who didn't get to the meeting on time or who left the lights on in the office last night. Usually it's more to do with perceived power over hidden issues such as pay, parking spaces, or promotions.

The more extreme the personality, the more careful you will have to be when interacting with that person. If you find yourself face to face with Godzilla in khakis or are the recipient of a nasty e-mail from Elvira down in accounting, the first thing to do is to decide whether the issue can be ignored or should be passed on up or down the line to a coworker or your boss. Never participate in any melodrama in which things tend to get personal. Keep everything on a professional level, and take all the time you need to prepare a careful, measured response that gets your side of the story across without escalating tensions between you and the Marquis de Sade.

Try to acknowledge your interest in resolving the problem at hand. If the aggressor continues to rant and rave, stop that person in his or her tracks simply by ending the conversation, adding that you'll be happy to continue the discussion when he or she calms down. Such a response places you in charge of the situation, sending a clear message to the aggressor that wild behavior is not acceptable and that you will no longer engage him or her on that basis. One tip is to pick someone out in the office who has demonstrated an ability to defuse tense situations and calmly handle office drama kings/queens. By observing a master of the craft, you can identify and employ the positive coping strategies that he or she uses when communicating with toxic coworkers.

Also, before you pass judgment on the office hothead or the workplace sycophant, try keeping an open mind, and remember that wonderful saying from the Sioux Indians that promises, "I will not judge my brother until I have walked two weeks in his moccasins."

THE 12 TYPES OF OFFICE PERSONALITIES

A big advantage in dealing with difficult coworkers comes with recognizing who they are and why they do the nasty things they do. As any battlefield commander will attest, understanding the enemy is the key to victory. Here are the big 12 troublesome office personalities and what to do about them.

The Steamroller

Rude and brutish, steamrollers don't care whose feelings they hurt or whose toes they step on. Lacking in the social graces, steamrollers more than compensate by engaging in behavior that a *Jerry Springer Show* contestant might describe as "tacky."

Response Mechanism

Nip steamrollers in the bud by telling them that you won't take their abuse. If they continue to attack and criticize, let them know that you'll go to their boss and then the boss's boss until their behavior stops. If they continue to attack, don't be reluctant to use the term *harassment* in response. There is no stronger word in the business lexicon these days. Management doesn't like rabble-rousers or anyone else whose actions border on harassment and will take the steps necessary to stop steamrollers from treading into that territory.

The Buck Passer

Negative to the core, buck passers are poisonous to your company and to your career. They are so unhappy with their jobs, their marriages, or their lives that they'll try to sink your morale, too.

Response Mechanism
Hold them accountable. If they respond to a request by repeating the buck passer's mantra, "It's not my job," remind them that it is their job and that you can't make progress on the project or program you're working on until they come through with the help you need. Be diplomatic, but be firm. With a buck passer, firmness is usually all it takes to get them off their backsides and into the game.

The Faultfinder

A common breed in Cubicle Nation, faultfinders will criticize everything you do and anything you say. Invariably they don't have workable solutions of their own.

Response Mechanism
Insist that faultfinders come up with a solution to the problem at hand. Ask them for an example or some direction. Ask them for details on why they disagree with you. Asking faultfinders to be specific usually reveals them to be the blowhards that they are. They're so busy bringing everyone down that they don't have the time or, more likely, the smarts to offer a better idea. Make them try.

The Obsessive-Compulsive

Also known as micromanagers or perfectionists, obsessive-compulsives will spend hours on the small picture and avoid the big picture altogether. Red pencil in hand, they will make your life miserable over misspelled words or out-of-place commas or quotation marks. The fact that you have an idea that can bring $1 million into your company's bank account will always be missed by obsessive-compulsives, who have got better things to do, like pointing out your grammar inadequacies or telling you to straighten your tie.

Response Mechanism
Avoid obsessive-compulsives if at all possible. If your boss is an obsessive-compulsive, then try to set ground rules early about what is realistic and what isn't. Don't worry too much about obsessive-compulsives. They find fault with everybody, so chances are you won't be alone as an object of their criticism.

The Monkey Wrencher

Always willing and able to gum up the works, monkey wrenchers don't like change and will do whatever they can to sabotage it. Monkey wrenchers usually are long-timers who are only too happy to regale you with tale after long-winded tale about the way "we used to do things."

Response Mechanism
Careful, savvy monkey wrenchers usually carry a company manual around with them to back up their arguments. However, if you're charged with changing a company process or policy and a monkey wrencher is standing in your way, stick to your guns, and show him that management is behind you. Again, be nice, but be

firm. Diplomacy goes a long way toward avoiding making enemies in the workplace.

The Sour Note

Also known as whiners or complainers, sour notes are never happy, and there's not much you can do to change their ways. You have to be careful with sour notes. They spread misery and kill morale—Johnny Appleseeds planting the seeds of frustration and hopelessness wherever they tread.

Response Mechanism

Thankfully, sour notes don't have to be taken too seriously. Even management recognizes sour notes and rarely puts them in positions of power. Take sour notes with a grain of salt—and don't become one.

The Rumormonger

The sky is falling! The sky is falling! Nobody likes bad news, real or imagined, more than rumormongers. Never in a position to create or verify news, rumormongers spread misinformation and fear wherever they go. The real problem is that sooner or later you can't believe anything rumormongers say.

Response Mechanism

Discount anything rumormongers say. Avoid rumormongers if you can, but if you have to deal with them, make it known to them that you don't have time to worry about things over which you have no control. Thus the latest rumor about the Japanese company buying your company out carries no water with you. After recognizing your noninterest, rumormongers will move on to a more eager listener. And whatever you do, don't discuss anything of importance with rumormongers—or known associates of rumormongers. If the office takes this attitude, rumormongers will starve for lack of information and cease to be a problem.

The Data Hoarder

Think of Wally in "Dilbert' and you have a good role model for data hoarders. They're tough to deal with because they usually do have good information that can move a project along at a nice, crisp pace. The trouble is that they don't want to share the information with anyone else, usually holding onto it until the time is right for the data to meet their own nefarious purposes. One example is the software engineer who's known about bugs in the new application software but won't say so until two weeks before performance reviews come out. Then he looks like a hero for saving the day.

Response Mechanism

Take data hoarders seriously. Better yet, take them out to lunch. The information they possess has value, and they know it. Therefore, trying to get on their good side and appealing to their human side—if there is one—is worth the effort. One thing is for sure. If you get on a data hoarder's bad side, you're cut off for good. Nothing short of an exorcism or a meeting with his supervisor will change this.

Mother/Father Superior

Mother/father superiors think that they walk on water and can do no wrong. However, mother/father superiors don't think the same about you or anyone else. Workplace know-it-alls are a challenge because, like data hoarders, they may have information they can use. Unlike data hoarders, however, who will keep the information to themselves, mother/father superiors will lord the information over you and try to make you feel inadequate for even asking.

Response Mechanism

Mother/father superiors often are overeducated types who lack the people skills to really get ahead in their careers. They don't buy into the old adage that anyone can be nice to a king, but it takes real class to be nice to a beggar. Not even in the same area code as "class," mother/father superiors commit the rest of their working lives to making others as miserable as they are. Try to humanize things and keep things light around mother/father superiors. Poke fun at yourself around them and satisfy their craving for superiority. It's no big deal for you because, unlike mother/father superiors, you're secure and comfortable with who you are. Mother/father superiors don't get invited to parties, and you do. They don't get plum assignments, and you do. In short, they don't have the basic ingredient that all chief executive officers (CEOs) love—the ability to get along with people.

The Victim

"It's all about me"—this sums up the workplace victim, who can never get enough sympathy or emotional nourishment from associates. There you are, minding your own business, whomping up a strategy for the next big meeting, and the victim appears at your desk, paperwork in hand, with a sob story on how overworked she is. The next thing you know, you've agreed to take some of the victim's workload just to get the victim to shut up and go away.

Response Mechanism

You can try ignoring victims, but this just makes them mad. How dare you go about your business when such an obvious injustice is taking place only a few cubicles away? Victims have been know to camp near employee workspaces overnight so that they can grab you as you walk in the door and bemoan their fate in life. One smart move is to outvictimize victims. If a victim is heading your way with a thick stack of folders and paperwork, head her off by moaning and groaning how busy you are and how unfair life is. This tactic usually confuses the victim, who will grow uncertain and move on to the next prospective victim, reluctant to ever return again.

The Pessimist

"Oh, woe is me! I'll never get a raise/vacation/promotion/parking space/key to the executive bathroom." So it goes with pessimists, close relatives of victims—only not as much fun to thwart. Pessimists are probably more dangerous than victims because the really good ones know how to plant seeds of doubt in your mind over workplace issues, such as an imminent move to Cleveland or the squashing of your department's budget. In addition, there are usually more than enough pessimists to go around, so they can work in pairs and double-team you with tales of dread and despair.

Response Mechanism

Perhaps the best move to make with pessimists is to arm yourself with facts and use them as bludgeoning tools to cripple their negativity. For example, if a coworker comes by saying that he can't possibly finish the project specs by next Friday, take 10 minutes and point out that the information needed to finish the task is easy to get. Point out where and how to get it. Whatever you do, don't give in and do the job yourself—this is what pessimists want. It might cost you a few minutes of your time, but given firm instructions, pessimists will be forced to dance to your music instead of the other way around.

The Overanalyzer

Overanalyzers are tough to combat because they prefer data to people. Overanalyzers procrastinate and obfuscate, driving the rest of the workplace bonkers with their inability to make a decision and move on. Content to work alone, surrounded only by computer spreadsheets and quantitative data software, overanalyzers try to pass themselves off as prudent and cautious members of the team, the last stopgaps between a big project's success and certain failure. In actuality, overanalyzers are gripped with paralysis at the thought of signing off on a decision and leaving their precious numbers and statistics to the wolves (meaning you and your associates).

Response Mechanism

Treat overanalyzers with kid gloves. Show respect for their work. Buy them the odd cup of coffee (just make sure it's not decaf—they are the ones you want to spur into action). A little encouragement will pry the information you need from overanalyzers. Overanalyzers don't like discouragement, though, and have been known to go into hiding for weeks on end if torched about their work on a recent project. The funny thing is that overanalyzers don't mind if they're criticized for dragging their feet. "Better to be safe than sorry," they will say with more than a hint of sanctimony. When all else fails, sic the steamroller on them—if there's one thing that overanalyzers hate more than being rushed, it's being threatened.

STAY ABOVE THE FRAY

In all these instances, certain rules apply to getting these troublemakers to sing from your hymnal. First, it is always important to keep the lines of communication open. Allow coworkers from hell to

Workplace No-No's

How can we avoid offending the people we work with? It seems as if this should be obvious. However, if it were, I wouldn't even be writing this chapter. Let's take a look now at actions that may offend your coworkers (in no particular order).

- Having loud telephone conversations
- Not cleaning up after yourself in the staff kitchen
- Showing up late for meetings
- Looking at a coworker's computer screen over his or her shoulder
- Taking supplies from a coworker's desk
- Neglecting to say please and thank you
- Wearing too much perfume or scent
- Chewing gum loudly
- Taking the last of something without replacing it
- Talking behind someone's back
- Asking someone to lie for you
- Blaming someone else when you are at fault
- Taking credit for someone else's work
- Asking a subordinate to do something unrelated to work, such as running errands
- Espousing your political or religious beliefs
- Opening someone else's mail
- Sending unwanted e-mail
- Telling offensive jokes
- Smoking in common areas
- Not pulling your own weight
- Complaining about the company, the boss, or coworkers
- Having a condescending attitude toward others

express their viewpoints—just make sure that you get your point across too (remember, politely, but firmly). It's also beneficial to hone your listening skills when dealing with difficult coworkers. There's a big difference between talking *with* someone and talking *to* them.

Some companies, in recognition of the rise in workplace confrontations, are turning to physical responses to calm everyone down. No, I don't mean hiring bouncers with Worldwide Wrestling Federation credentials, although that would be worth the price of admission. I mean things like allowing employees to receive a 10-minute massage while they sit at their desks. The reasoning is that a massage is relaxing and can change the sour mood of an employee to a content mood within a matter of minutes.

Some companies are also offering meditation rooms. According to the National Safety Council, 1 million employees are absent on any workday due to stress-related issues. To help employees cope with stress, employers have these rooms for their workers "to get away from it all." After relaxing in these rooms, which have dim lighting, comfortable chairs and couches, and most important, no telephones, employees return to their work areas feeling refreshed and reenergized. This is the idea anyway.

Other companies offer on-site workout facilities so that employees can perspire away their pent-up emotions on a treadmill or weight machine. Still others rely on weekly "Happy Hours," although I'm not sure plying a cubicle commando with alcohol will ever make it into the Harvard Business School handbook.

Ultimately, getting along with your coworkers is up to you. Sure, it requires some effort, and yes, you'll gag at the thought of appeasing some of the clods you call coworkers. At worst, however, it's a lesson in human relations that will encourage you to see another person's viewpoint, and at best, management will notice how well you play with others.

Above all, don't mind criticism. If it is untrue, disregard it. If it is unfair, don't allow it to irritate you. It if is ignorant, smile. If it is justified, learn from it.

What Type of Office Personality Are You?

This little test will be fun. Every office has its share of Neanderthals and ne'er-do-wells. To be fair, however, let's see how you measure up. Take this test to find out where you fit in the office ecosystem.

1. Your boss is giving a presentation to the 15 members of the board of trustees in 20 minutes. You notice a typo on page 5 of the 20-page document he or she will be handing out. You
   a. Call the boss's executive assistant and the intern who put the document together, scream at both of them for not catching the mistake, and then make them reprint 15 copies of page 5, unbind all 15 copies, and reinsert the new page 5 before the boss goes into the meeting.
   b. Reprint page 5 and unbind and reinsert the new page yourself, all the while telling everyone within earshot how you caught the executive assistant's mistake and that you are taking it on yourself to correct it.
   c. Whiteout the error on page 5 and write in the correct word using a felt-tip pen.
   d. Ignore it because nobody is going to read a 20-page document anyway.
2. When the practical joker in the office strikes, you
   a. Get angry with him and point out that he obviously doesn't have enough work to do.
   b. Are working so hard you don't even notice.

Continued

c.   Laugh along with the rest of the staff at the practical joke he played on you.

    d.   Get inspired to plan a practical joke of your own.

3. The information technology (IT) department is working on the network, which causes your computer to crash about every half hour. You

    a.   Call the vice president of information technology every time your computer goes down to complain because you don't have time for this.

    b.   Tell all your coworkers that you are saving every 5 minutes to deal with this burden and encourage them to do the same.

    c.   Run out of your office every time the network goes down yelling, "Is anyone else having computer problems?"

    d.   Stop working and make some personal phone calls.

4. The new summer intern is working on a document for you, but his computer skills are limited. When you get the first draft of the document, it is a total mess. The intern didn't even run Spell Check. You

    a.   Throw the document at the intern and loudly tell him to learn how to set up a document fast.

    b.   Rework the document yourself.

    c.   Waste an entire day helping the intern set up the document, even if you have work waiting on your desk.

    d.   Are happy that your workload has dropped off since he arrived.

5. The CEO has asked you to work on a last-minute project for him. It will require a lot of long days and weekend work. Your assistant has had a vacation scheduled for several months that now falls during the middle of the project. You

    a.   Tell your assistant to either cancel his plans or look for another job.

    b.   Tell your assistant that you can handle the extra work for one week and that he should just enjoy his vacation.

Continued

c.   Frantically ask anyone on your team if they could play assistant for you during that week.

    d.   Plan to call in sick that week.

6. A staff meeting is held at which you need to present some data, but you didn't have time to research your subject thoroughly. One of your coworkers challenges you during the meeting on a point you made. You

    a.   Begin attacking her credibility until she backs off.

    b.   Apologetically tell the staff that you will double-check your information and get back to them.

    c.   Agree with your coworker.

    d.   Tell the staff that you didn't have time to do your research very thoroughly because of all the other things you were working on.

7. A coworker has been out on maternity leave. When she brings the new baby in to meet the office staff, you

    a.   Congratulate her quickly and get back to your work.

    b.   Fuss over the baby while telling her your baby horror stories, i.e., "My sister's baby was so big that he got stuck on her pubic bone on the way out."

    c.   Excitedly run through the office to tell everyone to "come see our new employee."

    d.   Stay with her and the baby until she leaves.

8. The coworker who was out on maternity leave comes back to work. The staff decides to take her to lunch to celebrate her return. You

    a.   Eat lunch at your desk to get work done.

    b.   Go to lunch with them and tell your coworker to call you if she needs anything.

    c.   Go to lunch with them and tell your coworker that she should join the gym to get that baby weight off.

    d.   Go to lunch with them and have two beers.

Continued

9. A department director complains to your boss about something you did. Your boss calls you into her office to discuss the complaint. You
   a. Go back to your desk and enroll the complaining director onto 15 different Internet porn e-mail lists.
   b. Apologize repeatedly to your boss and offer to contact the director to apologize.
   c. Burst into hysterical tears.
   d. Think about something else as your boss talks.

10. Every time you deal with the receptionist in the human resources (HR) office, she treats you rudely and never answers your questions. You go to the HR office to get new forms, and the receptionist tells you that she doesn't have the forms you need and that you'll have to come back next week. You
    a. Make a scene and tell the receptionist that she should get off her fat butt and run new copies of the form.
    b. Thank the receptionist and tell her you'll try to get back there next week if you can.
    c. Tell the receptionist that you can't get back there next week because you'll be busy, that you need the forms now because the insurance company need the forms by Friday, and that if you don't get the forms, you will have all sorts of problems and…
    d. Thank the receptionist for being so rude and walk out.

Scoring

Count the number of times you chose each letter. If you chose one letter four times or more, you may be one of the following office types. Keep in mind that the more times you chose a specific letter, the more likely you are the type indicated; i.e., 10 *a*'s means you are a total psycho.

> *Four or more a's.* You are the office psycho. You work 16 hours a day every day, including weekends, in part because you

Continued

work inefficiently and do not manage your time well. You expect your coworkers to work the same way you do, including long days and weekends. You may be anal retentive and/or obsessive-compulsive, which you call "detail-oriented." You get angry easily and yell at everyone around you. You are probably a manager or director because your bosses appreciate your hard work. However, your coworkers probably hate you, and your staff would like to kill you. You probably have gone through several assistants throughout your career. Your behavior most likely has cost the company many good people who have left rather than continue working with you. Seek therapy! There is more to life than work.

Four or more b's. You are the office martyr, the patron saint of the office. You take on more than your fair share of the work, and then you let everyone know how long-suffering you are. Your coworkers come to you when they need a favor, and you always say yes, expecting them to return the favor, but they never do because you never ask. When you get angry, you show it in a passive-aggressive manner, never directly. You may feel unappreciated, and you probably are correct. You are probably frustrated because people expect so much more of you, but it is you who allows people to take advantage of you. As long as you continue to play martyr, nothing will ever change. Learn to say no and not feel guilty. Also, learn to talk yourself up.

Four or more c's. You are the office shrinking violet. When practical jokes are played in the office, you are usually the butt of those jokes. You have a tendency to say the first thing that comes to mind without thinking of the repercussions. You are probably an emotional person, and you react to every situation with open emotions. Your coworkers probably think that you are weird and may even think of you as incompetent no matter how good you are at your job. How your coworkers

Continued

view you can be important, especially if your company does peer reviews. Think more about the repercussions before you do or say something. And remember, the office is a political environment. Always put yourself in the best possible light.

Four or more d's. You are the office goof-off: When there is nothing to do, you are the first one to do it. You don't take the job very seriously, and as a result, your work is often late, sloppy, and full of mistakes. You fill a chair, and that is about it. For you, it is just a job. You probably don't make an effort to interact much with your coworkers because you don't really care to know those people. Your coworkers resent your laziness and complain to the boss often. You should always have a quick job lined up because chances are that you will be fired eventually.

If you (like me when I took this test) come up with a fairly even mix of all letters: You are human. Everyone has psycho days, martyr days, goof-off days, and shrinking-violet days. Just be aware of yourself, and always be willing to apologize to coworkers after you've had a bad day.

Office Lingo for the Twenty-First Century

Knowing and recognizing the various workplace personalities around you is a bit easier if you know the lingo. See if some of these definitions ring true at your company.

Adminisphere   Middle management: the rarified organizational layers beginning just above the rank and file. Decisions that fall from the adminisphere often are profoundly inappropriate or irrelevant to the problems they were designed to solve.

Continued

Assmosis　The process by which some people seem to absorb success and advancement by kissing up to the boss.

Beepilepsy　The brief seizure people sometimes suffer when their beepers go off, especially in vibrator mode. This is characterized by physical spasms, goofy facial expressions, and stopping speech in midsentence.

Blamestorming　Sitting around in a group discussing why a deadline was missed or a project failed and who was responsible.

Career-limiting move (CLM)　Used among microserfs to describe an ill-advised activity. Trashing your boss while he or she is within earshot is a serious CLM.

Chainsaw consultant　An outside expert brought in to reduce the employee head count, leaving the top brass with clean hands.

Cube farm　An office filled with cubicles.

Dilberted　To be exploited and oppressed by your boss. "I've been dilberted again. The old man revised the specs for the fourth time this week."

Flight risk　Used to describe employees who are suspected of planning to leave the company or department soon.

Glazing　Corporate-speak for sleeping with your eyes open at conferences and early-morning meetings. "Didn't he notice that half the room was glazing by the second session?"

G.O.O.D. job　A "get out of debt" job. A well-paying job people take in order to pay off their debts, one that they will quit as soon as they are solvent again.

High dome　Egghead, scientist, or Ph.D.

Idea hamsters　People who always seem to have their idea generators running.

Open-collar workers　People who work at home or telecommute.

Prairie-dogging　Something happens in a cube farm, and people's heads pop up over the walls to see what's going on.

Continued

Salmon day   Swimming upstream all day to get screwed in the end.

Seagull partner   A partner who flies in, makes a lot of noise, craps all over everything, and then leaves.

Strawman   A proposal everyone expects to fail but will still get your group noticed, as in "a strawman proposal for the marketing weenies."

Stress puppy   A person who thrives on being stressed out and whiny.

Tourists   Employees who take training classes just to take a vacation from their jobs. "We had three serious students in the class; the rest were tourists."

Triority   The three important things your boss expects you to do at once.

Xerox subsidy   Euphemism for swiping free photocopies from the workplace.

Reality Check: "Turfing" the Opposition

What do you do with a problem coworker who just refuses to get along with the group? If you can't get the person fired, at least get him or her transferred out of your department.

That's what coworkers Donna Bradley and Michelle Bowren did when a colleague's obnoxious behavior became too much to bear.

Senior planners at a catering and events company that helped companies run seminars, conferences, and other business meetings, 20-somethings Bradley and Bowren found themselves repeatedly tripped up by a marketing staffer who was routinely assigned to them. The staffer was argumentative, poorly prepared, and failed to respond to customer requests. The duo felt that they were getting the short end of the stick, and repeated complaints to management produced few results.

"The rumor was that she was the daughter of our founder's college roommate, so there was no way she was going to be fired," recalls Bradley.

"Donna and I were good friends, and we decided that we would take care of our 'problem' in a unique way as soon as an opportunity presented itself," added Bowren.

That opportunity came when the firm hired a new planner to handle a brokerage company's "road show"—a 10-city, two-month travel campaign to sell investors shares of a new stock it was underwriting. The campaign would be handled by the new planner who immediately established her operation as a top priority and commenced stepping on as many feet as she could to get all the resources she needed—and more—to handle the brokerage company job.

"This new planner rubbed us the wrong way from the start," says Bradley. "After one meeting, I looked at Michelle and we both knew that the new planner and our problem employee were made for each other." Acting with patience and care, the duo began dropping hints about the marketing fireball they had under their supervision and how she had "connections" with senior management. That's all the bait the new planner needed, and she immediately "turfed" Bradley and Bowren by scooping the disgruntled marketing staffer up for her team without so much as a phone call to another manager. "We made a show of protesting to enhance our credibility," says Bowren. "But behind closed doors we were high-fiving each other."

Back to business, the duo sailed on, unencumbered by the marketing staffer from Hell. Score one for the "turfed."

7

Crouching Boss, Hidden Agenda: How to Get Along with Your Boss

C an two coworkers get along without driving each other crazy? This is the question that frazzled employees ask each other after their latest confrontation with the boss.

Okay, some people don't like the term *boss,* preferring a terrain-leveling moniker such as *coach* or *manager.* Even *supervisor* makes the cut. And employees really aren't *employees* anymore. They are *associates, team members,* or *co-owners.*

Maybe this is why so many employee-boss relations go sour—nobody knows what to call each other these days.

Whatever you call the person you answer directly to at work—and since this is a family-oriented book, let's keep it clean—few people have more influence over your career's fortune than your boss, that noted dispenser of raises and promotions. A good boss knows you, knows your work, and knows your strengths and weaknesses. A good boss provides guidance and direction, can communicate directives clearly, and then steps out of the way so that you can do your job. There's a great story about the time that Henry Ford hired an efficiency expert to go through his plant. He said, "Find the nonproductive people. Tell me who they are, and I will fire them!" The expert made the rounds with his clipboard in hand and finally returned to Henry Ford's office with his report. "I've found a problem with one of your administrators," he said. "Every time I walked by, he was sitting with his feet propped up on the desk. The man never does a thing. I definitely think you should consider getting rid of him!" When Henry Ford learned the name of the man the expert was referring to, Ford shook his head and said, "I can't fire him. I pay that man to do nothing but think—and that's what he's doing."

A good boss also can help you get ahead in your career by going to bat for you with a recommendation for promotion or write a glowing reference for you for a position at another company. He or she also can encourage you to live your dreams. A friend of mine once decided to take a sabbatical to sail a small boat across the Atlantic Ocean. While his family and friends grew pessimistic and fretted over his odds of completing the journey safely, his boss encouraged him, saying, "You can do this," and "I believe in you." The boss knew the golden rule of employee management—to offer encouragement that the seemingly impossible can be achieved.

A good boss also can provide inspiration and challenge you to meet and surpass the career goals you've established for yourself. When young F. W. Woolworth was a store clerk, he tried to convince his boss to have a 10-cent sale to reduce inventory. The boss agreed, and the idea was a resounding success. This inspired Woolworth to open his own store and price items at a nickel and a dime. He needed capital for such a venture, so he asked his boss to supply the capital for part interest in the store. His boss turned him down flat. "The idea is too risky," he told Woolworth. "There are not enough items to sell for 5 and 10 cents." Woolworth went ahead without his boss's backing, and not only was he successful in his first store, but eventually he also owned a chain of F. W. Woolworth stores across the nation. Later, his former boss was heard to remark, "As far as I can figure out, every word I used to turn Woolworth down cost me about a million dollars."

DYSFUNCTION JUNCTION

The trouble is that there are as many bad bosses as good ones.

Bad bosses hurt careers. They try to steal credit for things you do. They try to undermine you and make you doubt your worth to the company. They lie to you and try to chisel away at your vast reservoir of goodwill. Bad bosses are ignorant, too. Some have to wear drool buckets in public, yet they'll assume intellectual superiority over you just the same.

The worse thing about bad bosses is that they do all these evil things and still sleep well at night.

What bad bosses don't—or can't—realize is that their arrogance and bungling management styles hurt their companies, hurt their employees, and ultimately hurt themselves. There's a great "Dilbert" cartoon about the pointy-headed boss sending new hire Albert Einstein packing because he isn't a team player. "Dilbert" is so hilarious because creator Scott Adams hits so close to home. We've all had bosses who would send an Albert Einstein packing and not think a thing of it.

Thus with so much at stake in an employee-manager relationship, you'd think that both parties would go out of their way to get along with one another. Unfortunately, many employee-boss relationships run closer to the Captain Queeg and Fletcher Christian variety than they do to the Ozzie and Harriet style.

For proof, look no further than the cottage industry of complaint-oriented Web sites that has sprung up in recent years. These sites allow workers to blast their bosses online without fear of reprisal. Sites like mybosssucks.com, iquit.com, and F*****dcompany.com draw tons of traffic, so obviously these and other online forums have struck a nerve with the working public.

Some sites specialize in taunting bosses. For example, iquit.com will send your boss a form letter that begins with such phrases as "Dear Sir/Madam: You are an idiot, and I can prove it." And the site will do it for $1.

Company-specific sites also have sprung up that let staffers complain about bosses. These include such sites as the Disgruntled Burger King Employee Page, FaceIntel.com, and yes, the Disgruntled Postal Worker Zone.

A word to the wise: Some companies are fighting back by sending armies of lawyers after the owners of these Web sites and Web portal giants, such as Yahoo.com. They want and often get the identities of Internet flamers who slam their bosses, often with some embellishment that doesn't survive the harsh light of the U.S. justice system. Some people have lost their jobs as a result and face hefty fines for libeling their managers.

GIT ALONG, LI'L DOGGIES

Why waste all that negative energy, which accomplishes nothing, when you can develop some solid communication skills that will allow you not only to get along with your boss but also to leverage the relationship for your career gain?

Try the following tips to see if they don't help you forge better ties with your boss. At the very least, they should reduce the urge to jeopardize your career by slamming him on an online forum that's being monitored by your employer.

Make the Boss Look Good

I know, I can hear your teeth grinding from here. But if you think about it, the best way to achieve harmony and position yourself for a big raise or promotion is to do your job well. If your boss is given a set of goals from her boss and you help your boss reach those goals, chances are that everyone goes home happy. How do you do this? By . . .

> *Understanding what your boss wants.* Bosses are like dogs, only not as easy to paper train and more likely to drop a Frisbee when you fling one at them. As in training a dog, you have to develop a knack for reading their minds and recognizing what they want. Some employees drift through careers because they overlook their bosses' signals. If your reports are first-rate but include the odd spelling error, a particularly anal boss will likely focus on your inattention to detail rather than on your compelling grasp of nuclear fission. Consequently, don't assume that things are okay because you know your stuff. Pay attention to whatever feedback you are getting from your manager, and address any concerns right away.

Again, the notion of accommodating a particularly loath-some manager's obsession for double spacing and Helvetica fonts understandably may tighten your colon and cause you to buy Motrin by the ton, but don't think short term. Think long term. Do good work and appease the ogre by aug-menting that work with an understanding of how he wants it presented. A master chef knows that cooking a mouth-watering dish is only half the battle—preparing and pre-senting it in an eye-pleasing manner should close the deal. The same is true with bosses.

One other thing: When you understand your boss, you can begin anticipating what he wants. And anticipating what management wants is the Holy Grail of the employee-boss relationship. Once you do that, it won't be long before peo-ple will be running around trying to figure out what you want.

Keeping your boss in the loop. It is common courtesy to keep bosses apprised of a project's progress. In fact, your future relies on your ability to keep your manager in the loop. Why? Because bosses don't like a lot of things, but surprises and embarrassment are at the top of the list. If things are going well, a short conversation or e-mail should suffice. If a prob-lem arises, get it all down on paper in a memo explaining the problem and (ideally) offering some solutions.

Whatever you do, don't try to hide a problem. Let your manager know as soon as possible that you have a serious problem. Tell your manager what solutions you propose, and ask for any additional recommendations. You'll be surprised at how supportive your manager will be. After all, it's her neck on the bottom line, too.

Not wasting your boss's time. In the information age, time is money, and time wasted is money you can never get back. Of course, much depends on your relationship with your boss. This said, even the best of relationships shouldn't include a running account of your keg party the weekend before and—God forbid—a timetable to pay back the bail money your boss lent you. Think of time with your boss as currency. You've only got a limited amount of currency to spend, so choose your time with him or her wisely. And don't be in your boss's office complaining all the time. You'll be judged by the solutions you bring to the table—not the problems.

Also remember that there are a myriad of people just like you reporting to the same manager. Before going in, write down what you need to discuss and what you need from your boss.

Be ready to answer simple questions. When you have what you need, it's time to leave—unless the boss wants to discuss something more with you. Then follow up your meeting in writing, unless your boss tells you directly not to. A short memo outlining what was discussed and what actions you both agreed to take should do the trick.

Also try to determine whether your boss is what management guru Peter Drucker calls a "reader" or a "listener." In other words, how does your boss best receive information? Via written or oral presentation? Brief or detailed? The implications, according to Drucker, are clear. If your boss is a reader, send a written report first, and follow it up with a face-to-face discussion. If your boss is a listener, brief him or her on the subject or make a presentation, depending on the boss's preference, and then send a written report afterward.

Being a rock. Be dependable, and be reliable (it's your turn to be the dog). Show up early and hit your deadlines. Volunteer for work when you've got the free time. It makes the day go by faster and earns you a great deal of respect from management.

Not taking criticism personally. Nobody likes to be criticized, fairly or not. But when your boss points out that the budget numbers you crunched are wrong and takes the time to explain why, listen. Take notes—but don't take it personally. Biting your lips, clenching your fists, and turning the color of a fire truck are only going to breed resentment all around. Keep an open mind. Most bosses want you to do well. If they don't, it reflects poorly on them. If they're ham-handed or cruel in their feedback, let them know you have an open mind and want to learn but that you don't respond well to personal attacks. Always stand up for yourself. If an insecure boss thinks that he can get away with badgering you or cutting you to ribbons over a mistake, he'll continue to do so until you speak up. Firmly but politely say, "I don't appreciate your hostility. Feel free to provide feedback but keep it professional."

Not playing games. Almost nothing will sink you faster with management than playing politics on the job. Criticizing a coworker or passing along second-hand information on a coworker is a big mistake. First, it puts your loyalty to the company in question. Remember the line about how loose lips sink ships? Second, it takes up time your boss is being paid to use elsewhere—a fact he will remember. Lastly, a boss will question the seriousness and professionalism of a person who keeps poking his nose into other people's business. And a person who's perceived as being unprofessional and not serious can kiss career advancement prospects good-bye.

Thinking partnership. No, not as an official partner of the firm—at least not yet. Think of your relationship with your manager as a partnership in which you each give a little to get a lot. By definition, partnerships involve mutual respect and trust. These are the attributes you really want in a relationship with a person who holds so much influence over your career.

Knowing your boss's quirks. What is your boss's pet peeve? What brings a smile to her face? How does your boss view the industry and your company's role in it? Does she like to be reached by e-mail, phone, memo, or an office visit? Does she like to get a detailed report, or will bullet points suffice? Every manager is different. Get to know the differences in your boss, and accommodate them.

Going ahead and pitching ideas. Some bosses are so insecure that they can't handle someone they perceive to be more intelligent than they are. Most bosses aren't like this, however, and will welcome your ideas as long as they

- Are well reasoned
- Are solution-oriented to a specific company problem
- Make them look good
- Have the best interests of the company at heart
- Don't add to the workloads of others while not adding to yours

THE SEVEN TYPES OF BOSSES

I don't know if you had fun reading about the 12 types of coworkers in Chapter 6, although I hope that you found it instructive. I had so much fun writing it, however, that I want to do the same here to help you identify the seven types of bosses.

Just as being able to identify the different types of coworkers makes you more effective in dealing with them adeptly and thus raising your own profile in the workplace, so too is there immense value in knowing who your boss is and what makes him tick—or detonate, for that matter.

The Huckster

Call them shameless, call them credit-grabbers, call them self-promoters, just don't call a huckster before you claim credit for your hard work on the big project. The huckster will elbow you out of the way and crowd you and your coworkers out of the limelight.

Response Mechanism

It's okay to edge your boss into the limelight a little bit, but it's not okay for your boss to hog all the credit. Don't let your boss get away with it. Put your name on all your work—reports, white papers, memos, and project updates. In this way, when the project is over, people will recognize that your name was all over it from the get-go. Don't, however, become a huckster yourself. Only claim credit for the work you've done—word will get around when you take more credit than you deserve, and it won't reflect well on you.

The Good Buddy

Who's your buddy? Who's your pal? Trust me, it's not this guy. While he's busy slapping you on the back and telling you what a great job you're doing, you're not really getting the solid feedback you need to improve your job skills. The trouble with these happy-go-lucky types is that there's usually no substance there. And their management skills are only skin deep. It is better to have a drill sergeant who helps you improve and deliver results.

Response Mechanism
Take the good buddy in stride, but don't count on much hands-on management. These types don't change their stripes and probably will look at you funny if you ask for an honest assessment of your job performance. Instead, pick a coworker you like and respect, and trade information together. Analyze each other, and act as one another's manager. It will be great preparation for the day when you do become the boss.

The Glub-Glubber

Glub-glubbers are managers who are in over their heads—only they seem to be the last to know it. It is frustrating knowing more about your department, your company, or your industry than your boss does, but it's a fact of life in a fast-paced work culture where reorganizations occur with the frequency of a new Starbucks opening in your neighborhood. Not knowing where to turn and afraid to admit that they are stumped, glub-glubbers invariably will make bad decisions. Glub-glubbers tend to hire employees who are either too strong or too weak and either push employees too hard or not all. Why? Because they have no clue. You have to be careful with glub-glubbers. Ambitious employees are threatening to them. And if you make them look too good, they will grab you in a Vulcan death grip and never allow you to leave the department.

Response Mechanism
Glub-glubbers will flinch at the first sign of being exposed as the frauds and charlatans they are. Of course, then they are just pathetic.

Let them know that you are sympathetic to their plight and will try to help bring them up to speed. Offer to help them prepare, and accompany them to big meetings. Offer to create a departmental manual. However, because they will benefit from this knowledge, there has to be something in it for you, too. Suggest a new title or a new desk near a window or an office if one is available. Insist that you get credit for your work—unscrupulous glub-glubbers will hog all the credit and run. If you're nice and helpful to glub-glubbers, you can at least expect a glowing recommendation that you can bring to your new position higher up in the firm.

The Type A

Cartoonist Matt Groenig, creator of *The Simpsons*, pegs type A's as cold-hearted tyrants who go around threatening employees with lines like, "How dare you duck when I throw things at you?" or "I don't pay you to think; I pay you to cringe while I rant and rave." This about sums the type A up.

Response Mechanism

When you draw the short straw and get the type A, there's really not much you can do but ride out the storm. Thankfully, in this day and age of harassment claims, workplace tyrants can't go over the line. Just keep your wits about you and your head down, and do your job (which is good advice for any employee). You can try to pacify type A's by appealing to their ego by offering to byline an article in an industry trade publication or promote them for an industry award, but don't go overboard. With bullies like these, your best bet is to respect yourself and demand respect from them as well. Like most bullies, they don't like being pushed back.

The Anal-Retentive

Anal-retentives are perfect and want to know why you can't be perfect too. Often absorbed in the details, anal-retentives don't see the big picture and therefore are a danger to your career advancement campaign, which always has the big picture as a cornerstone. If you work for an anal-retentive, be prepared for little lectures on punctuation and long-winded narratives on company policy. Some anal-retentives have value in that they can help you become aware of your possible inattention to detail or your penchant for overlooking the company dress code.

Response Mechanism

Anal-retentives are nitpickers, true. However, try to keep an open mind and see if you can learn something from them. If you're as disorganized and a slacker to detail as I am, there's a lot to absorb from anal-retentives. One exasperated boss told me to go out and buy one of those notebook calendars so that I wouldn't forget about meetings and such. I still use the calendar today, and it's been a big help to me. In addition—and I don't know why this is—anal-retentives are the nicest people when you no longer work for them. Maybe it's because you're not in each other's faces over such earth-shaking issues as the dangling participle you used in that last memo or the amount of paper you wasted at the copier machine.

The Company Boss

Think Ward Cleaver from *Leave It to Beaver* or Monica Geller from *Friends*. Actually, most managers fit into this category, and this is not a bad thing. Decent folks by nature, they've had some power thrust on them and will be damned if they will allow that power to be taken away. They arrive early, stay late, and subscribe to all the pertinent industry publications. They're political animals who aren't above playing subordinates against each other to get the desired result. They're demanding but usually fair. They hustle because they have to; company bosses usually don't bring an overabundance of intellect to the position, so they compensate with hustle and a strong work ethic.

Response Mechanism

By and large, if you take care of the company boss, then the company boss will take care of you.

The Procrastinator

Saving procrastinators for last is appropriate because saving things until the last minute is what procrastinators do. Most workplace observers spend time admonishing staffers that waiting until the last minute to complete a task is a sign of laziness or poor time management skills. This may be true in some cases, but my experience is with procrastinators in management positions. You know how they operate. A directive hits their desk on Monday with a Friday deadline. Tuesday and Wednesday roll by, and still the directive just sits. They are too busy and too important to walk it over to you or send you an e-mail. Thursday comes and goes, and still no action. Finally, on Friday at 4:30 P.M., procrastinators notice the directive and drop it off on your desk—or more accurately, they have someone do it for them. "Take care of this before you go home today," says the note paper-clipped to the directive. The result: an urge to kill, followed by a mad scramble to change your plans for the evening and then a series of rushed calls and e-mails across the company looking for the information you need to complete the task. Coworkers roll their eyes in sympathy, but there's not much they can do.

Response Mechanism

I had a procrastinator for a boss once. We used to joke that his favorite animal was the turtle and that his favorite home appliance was a slow cooker. He would hold action items until late in the day before shipping them off to us hapless underlings, who would be forced to stay late and get the job done. I brought this habit up once, but he brushed it off, saying, "Hey, better late than never." As if this made his procrastination excusable.

Later that year we took up a collection and bought him a day timer and left it on his desk. We would have sprung for a watch, too, if we thought it would make a difference. However, the best way to handle these types is to nip this behavior in the bud. If your boss repeatedly hands you action items that have a deadline of under two hours or so, stand firm and say that you need more time to complete the task effectively. Don't yell, don't bite your lower lip, and don't back off, because your boss will take it as a sign of weakness and continue to take advantage of you. Be professional, and be polite. Ask to speak to your boss privately so that the possibility of embarrassing him or her in front of your coworkers is eliminated. Two things can happen in this instance. One, your boss will get mad at you and tell you to complete the damn assignment. This is not likely, though, if you're a good, well-respected employee of the firm, especially if you've enlisted coworkers to stand with you against time tyrants. The second option, much more likely, results in your boss's giving you more time to complete the directive.

One more thing: Use your judgment when you decide to speak up. If the company's stock price is in freefall after your chief executive officer (CEO) was found running down Market Street in a garter belt and panty hose singing the Dutch national anthem and your boss wants you to whip up a quick press release with the proper spin, do it. However, if it's a request to type up the corporate newsletter at 4:45 P.M. on a Friday, then stand your ground and make yourself heard.

HOW TO ASK YOUR BOSS FOR A REFERENCE

In the end game, you and your boss won't last forever. In some cases this is a shame, but in many cases it's not. Sooner or later you'll move on or he'll move on, and life will begin anew somewhere else.

When you do part ways—and it doesn't matter who leaves first—make sure you get a reference in your back pocket before you bid each other adieu.

A reference does some great things for you career-wise. It gives a future hiring manager a chance to review a peer's opinion of you, instead of your opinion of yourself (which is what your résumé does). Bosses consider themselves part of an exclusive club (or cult, if you're a cynic). They go off to conventions and wink and nod and exchange weird handshakes with each other like drunken fraternity brothers. This is fine. Just use this camaraderie as leverage for yourself with a reference letter, because they do like to read each other's correspondence.

Assuming that one of you is leaving (I wouldn't advise asking your boss for a reference if she doesn't know you're leaving), unless your boss is a real Gila monster, you should have no problem getting a reference. Something written is preferred, because that way you know what your boss is saying about you. The best way to ask depends on your relationship with your manager and on how she prefers to be contacted. If you can walk up to your boss on a regular basis to discuss company issues, then chances are that you can walk up to her and ask for a reference. A more distant boss might appreciate it if you ask for an appointment first.

Also, don't be reluctant to call on other company managers for references. All those task forces and team projects give you a chance to strut your stuff for many different managers. Cultivate those relationships, because they can give you additional reference options and maybe even lead you to a saner boss without your having to leave your company. The same goes for clients and vendors too. I once received a great letter of reference from an old corporate client. She was "glad to do it." Most decent people are.

HOW TO ASK YOUR BOSS FOR A RAISE

The days of walking into the boss's office and asking for a raise are becoming as rare as the three-martini lunch. The business world has increasingly turned to the annual review as a mechanism for discussing raises with the rank and file.

However, there are ways of cranking up your salary without having to wait for December to roll around.

The first thing you have to do is build a business case for your raise. Have you contributed to your department's success? Have you learned a new software program? Have you found a way to cut fat from the budget? Have you brought a new client in-house? Make a list of your accomplishments, and make a date to see your boss. Slip the list under your boss's nose. Remember, professionals always make requests in writing with backup.

If you are perceived as someone the company would prefer not to lose, you might get the raise. However, even if you don't get the raise, there could be other issues involved that have nothing to do you, such as a tight budget or a company-wide cap on salary increases.

If you don't get the raise, try not to get visibly upset about it. Nobody likes a whiner. Still, feel free to start shopping your services around to other companies. Many a raise request that was stamped "rejected" is suddenly stamped "accepted" when you have another job offer in your back pocket.

LASTLY, STAND UP FOR YOURSELF

With all types of bosses, know that you have a leg to stand on if you find you're being mistreated. If, for example, your boss keeps grabbing all the credit for your projects, make sure that you bring it up at your periodic review. Many firms these days have "open appraisal" reviews, where other managers are brought in so that you can speak your mind without fear of reprisal. If you plan on taking a credit-grabber on, be prepared with facts. Build a coalition of coworkers who feel the same way you do. There is strength in numbers. Coalitions are especially easy to create when issues such as late hours come up. Nobody wants to be at the office at 9 P.M., so if your boss keeps scheduling meetings and demanding that you work late, a group of like-minded staffers can make your case for earlier exit times that much stronger.

Above all, make sure that you let your boss know that you bring a lot to the table. A manager who knows an employee's value is a manager who invariably will reward that employee when raises, bonuses, promotions, and the like come rolling around.

Think aggressively. Create a personal file that contains notes, copies of awards, and recognition statements. Be sure that each item is dated, includes the name of the person for whom the work was done, and if possible, an estimate of the financial impact.

People who don't take the time to record what they have done are unable to recall their accomplishments. This penalizes them when times get tight and they have to fight to keep their present jobs or find others. Also keep records on how your suggestions, actions, and efforts have saved time, money, and material. Each time you accomplish a savings, note it, and give a copy of the note to your boss. By doing so, you demonstrate your value, remind your boss that you are working for the good of the organization, and establish a permanent reference that you can use.

This kind of productive relationship is much better than the debilitating one where you're ducking flying coffee mugs by day and crying into your pillow by night.

Matt Groenig's "Nine Types of Bosses"

The Angry Behemoth

"I don't pay you to think. I pay you to cringe while I scream and rant." This type is also known as the ape, Mr. Tantrum, grumpy, the grouch, and ol' flaring nostrils.

How to Handle
Hide, make snickering remarks to coworkers.
Warning: This is type is stupider [*sic*] than he looks.

The Robot from Planet X

"Your 10-minute break is over in 5 minutes." This type is also known as the bureaucrat, the watcher, the thing with the x-ray eyes, the living dead, the ice machine, and the zombie (or zombina).

How to Handle
Conceal all feelings.
Warning: This type is contagious.

Continued

Mr. Softy

"Gosh, I don't know about that. I'll just have to think about it for a while. I just. . . ." This type is also known as what's-its-name, squishy, the pushover, jellyfish, and moving target.

How to Handle

Gently.

> *Warning:* This type causes drowsiness.

The Slippery Eel

"Just keep quiet and do your job, and 12 to 24 months from now I think you're due for a surprise. No promises." This type is also known as the manipulator, the liar, the sneak, and the genius.

How to Handle

Run for your life.

> *Warning:* This type is everywhere.

The Great Unknown

This type is also known as the lurking unknown, the creeping unknown, and the hiding unknown.

How to Handle

Watch and wait.

> *Warning:* This type bites when cornered.

The Spitting Cobra

"Good morning. What an ugly shirt. It figures. Oh, cheer up." This type is also known as the snapping turtle, poison ivy, the pesky irritant, and oh no.

How to Handle

Boil with rage (silently).

> *Warning:* Your head may explode.

Continued

The Horny Toad

"Let's forget about work and just relax. How about a little drink? This could be your big break. Just kidding. Jeez, relax." This type is also known as sleazebucket, slimeball, scumbag, and the handsome devil.

How to Handle

Say forget it.
Warning: This could result in termination or, worse, marriage.

Wonder Boss

"Good news everyone. Because of a great year of fun and profits, I have hefty bonuses and a generous profit-sharing plan for all of you!" This type is also known as I don't believe it, god, perfection, and what a guy (or gal).

How to Handle

Throw caution to the wind.
Warning: This type could be the slippery eel in disguise.

The Psychotic Boss-Monster from Hell

"How *dare* you duck when I throw things at you!" This type is also known as the rampaging beast-thing, unreasonable, here comes trouble, and yessir, right away sir.

How to Handle

Cower and hope for a heart attack.
Warning: Don't let this type see this page.

(from *Work is Hell*)

REALITY CHECK: FLIGHT SCHOOL: TEACHING A NEW BOSS SOME OLD TRICKS

For Gene Atwell, airline public relations coordinator, dealing with the public and the press leaves little room for dealing with an inexperienced boss.

"I had enough on my plate," says the gregarious 36-year-old PR specialist. "But when I met my new staff director, I saw right away that I'd have to clear more room."

The problem? Atwell's new boss had no public relations experience—or customer service relations experience, for that matter. "He was a decent guy, but he came from management and had a management persona," says Atwell. "He rarely had to deal with the outside world. So when the calls starting coming in from the magazines and newspapers, or when he had to attend a ribbon-cutting ceremony and introduce our CEO in front of 2000 people, he had that 'deer in the headlights' look about him."

Atwell had two choices: not deal with the inexperienced boss and deal with his own job, or help the new guy along and try to make himself look good in the process. "I decided to approach him and offer my help—very diplomatically, of course," explains Atwell. "It wasn't like I was lording my experience over him, but I did make it clear that I could help him get up and running a lot quicker than if he tried to go it alone."

A crash course on dealing with people and the press followed. Atwell would have his boss sit in on conference calls and media interviews and learn how they were done. He also showed him how to create a press release with maximum impact. He sold his boss on the importance of community outreach and how to appease all parties involved.

"Before long he started climbing out of his shell and became more comfortable," adds Atwell. "Right away he started cutting me slack and offering me perks like time off when I needed it and giving me the choice airline conference assignments in Las Vegas and London. It was his way of saying thanks, I guess."

8

They Shoot Troublemakers, Don't They? The Fine Art of Managing Office Politics

---

Rare is the career professional who hasn't lost a job, a promotion, or a raise because of office politics. Possibly you've been blindsided by a treacherous boss who's resentful that your college degree overwhelms his or her high-school education. Or you've been stabbed in the back by a vengeful coworker whose romantic advances you rejected.

Hey, office politics happen.

Someone once said that a workplace is like a fishbowl—everyone who cares to look, both inside the company and out (people such as clients, vendors, and competitors), can see what's going on. I like this analogy and would take it a bit further. Actually, a workplace is like a giant aquarium, with sharks (of the basking and hammerhead varieties mostly), blowfish, suckers, remoras, jellyfish, bottom-dwellers, and other diverse species. Put all these and other aquatic animals in a giant aquarium and watch the water turn red with blood and torn body parts.

Like a seal that climbs onto an ice floe to avoid being the main dish for a killer whale, however, you can't isolate yourself from your coworkers and become an outsider. Sure, we'd all like to stay above the fray and be judged on our own accomplishments. But separating yourself from the pack isn't that easy. For that matter, it's not really advisable.

The fact is that people adept at the art of office politics are the ones who get ahead.

A recent study found that people who get on at work—earning promotions, pay raises, perks, and praise—are good at playing the office politics game. The same survey found that 95 percent of employees believe that politics plays some part in every working day. Every time we attend a meeting or are up against a deadline, we are caught up in workplace politics.

As I've said earlier, management often judges the value of an employee just as much on his or her people skills as it does on smarts or reliability. Managers know that there is no avoiding interaction with other workers, as much as we might think that we can by hiding behind e-mails, answering machines, and telecommuting tools. The real lifeblood of any business is the people who operate in it. Mingling with coworkers at the coffee machine or having a beer with a sales guy after work is much more than just a break from work—it's an opportunity to gain insider knowledge that can help you better navigate the rough seas of the corporate world.

Sure, much of what passes for office politics is distasteful. For instance, many rank-and-file workers dismiss the art of schmoozing or what some call "flatteratio"—the idle chitchat, small talk, lame jokes, and phony-laugh stuff—as a waste of time. Often it's not. In fact, a good argument can be made that not schmoozing is what keeps you outside a corner office and inside a cubicle. Personality is a big plus in business, sometimes a bigger factor than performance. Who among us hasn't worked for a boss who lacks the job skills we possess and probably the smarts too? Chances are that the boss grabbed the brass ring by demonstrating personal skills that endeared him to the higher-ups and muckety-mucks. He went to the company picnic and organized the softball game—making sure that he chose the sides. He was unafraid to engage the top brass in chitchat on the elevator. He could handle himself if the conversation turned away from the workplace and onto other topics, such as the Celtics-Lakers game that night or the new van Gogh exhibit down the street at the art museum. He had the *cojones* to invite the big kahunas to play golf with him. True, it's flattery, but there's a bit more to it than that. Company chief executive officers (CEOs) like to think of their employees as members of a community—family, if you will. And they like nothing better than happy, gregarious employees who enjoy being active contributors to that community in ways that go beyond performance on the job.

Understanding office politics as a means of climbing the career ladder is just the tip of the iceberg. This is going on offense, in football lingo. But you've got to play defense, too. If someone is taking potshots at you behind your back or plotting to exclude you from the big project, you want to have this knowledge and be able to fight back. Keeping yourself sealed off from coworkers means that you'll never get this knowledge and thus never know what hit you when bad news arrives at your desk. Let's make sure that this doesn't happen to you.

Different Worlds

How do employees and management view office politics. And do their views clash? More than a third (36 percent) of employees polled by OfficeTeam, an employee staffing service, said that the level of office politics has increased greatly compared with five years ago. But when asked the same question in a separate survey, only 12 percent of executives noted such a rise.

The poll of workers includes responses from 720 men and women, all 18 years of age or older and employed. One-hundred and fifty executives with the nation's 1000 largest companies were surveyed separately. Respondents were asked, "In your opinion, has the level of office politics in the workplace increased or decreased compared with five years ago?"

Employee responses:

- Increased greatly—36 percent
- Increased somewhat—34 percent
- Neither increased nor decreased—8 percent
- Decreased somewhat—10 percent
- Decreased greatly—4 percent
- Don't know/no answer—8 percent

Executive responses:

- Increased greatly—12 percent
- Increased somewhat—29 percent
- Neither increased nor decreased—38 percent
- Decreased somewhat—17 percent
- Decreased greatly—4 percent
- Don't know/no answer—0 percent

"Many executives are somewhat removed from the day-to-day conflicts that can arise between employees and therefore may not be fully aware of challenges that can exist," said Diane Domeyer, executive

Continued

director of OfficeTeam. To gain a better understanding of their firm's work environment, she encourages managers to observe it from their employees' perspective: What challenges are they under? Is the level of internal competition healthy or detrimental to productivity?

Domeyer noted that greater productivity demands facilitated by advanced technology have resulted in a rise in the number of self-managed and cross-functional work groups. While companies are seeing the benefits of this team structure, it also can become fertile ground for differences of opinion and personality conflicts among workers. She offers the following suggestions to help minimize the impact of office politics:

- *Reward team results.* Publicly recognize groups as well as individuals to motivate and inspire. Praising the entire team reinforces the message that collaboration is integral to success.

- *Maintain an open-door policy.* Be sure that employees feel comfortable sharing their concerns with management. Clear, two-way communication can help identify and diffuse potentially serious conflicts.

- *Avoid creating the "lone superstar."* The strongest individual achievers also should be able to work well with others. Make sure that the rules of business etiquette apply to all employees equally, regardless of status. "It's not my job" attitudes lie at the root of many politically charged situations.

- *Take active steps to gauge morale.* Check in with employees regularly and offer your help in solving problems. Political issues take a toll on employee morale and ultimately can lead to higher staff turnover.

PLUGGING INTO OFFICE POLITICS

The good news is that there is an art to office politics and it's easy to learn. There is a way to enjoy favorable relationships with your peers without being offended or alienated—without being judgmental or biased. You can be well respected and admired in the office without having to get down in the muck and begin slinging mud around. People like people who, instead of looking for others to blame, look instead for people to congratulate. That's the end game. That's where you want to be in your career. And here's how to do it.

Preparing to Play the Game

There are a few things to keep in mind before you kick things off.

Think Win-Win

Some workplace observers say that the only way to win the game of office politics is to make sure that the other guy loses. They say that office politics is a competition where people square off against one another until there's only one combatant left standing.

I don't buy it. Yes, you can play the game like this, but there's a heavy price to be paid for both winner and loser. The winner will be held accountable down the line because the vanquished have long memories and will want to balance the books by getting revenge. If Tanya in sales initiates a power play and grabs some of Bob's territory, Bob's not going to forget it. Sooner or later, he'll launch an offensive on his own at Tanya's expense.

It is better to engage in situations where everyone wins. If Tanya wants some of Bob's territory, she can offer to trade some territory of her own, perhaps with a fistful of sales leads in the process.

Don't Use Office Politics as a Crutch

Some people who get passed over for promotions or lose out on a corner office blame office politics. "I was a great fit for that vice president's position, but I didn't get it because of politics," is a common refrain. All too often the real reason is different. Maybe the employee didn't have the right experience for the job or was kept in her slot because that's what the company needed at the time. People who blame office politics for their workplace woes miss a good chance at self-examination. Facing the truth isn't easy. People don't want to think they don't fit the bill, but a hard look at the situation will reveal truths from which one can learn—and benefit—later on.

Prepare for the Political

During your career there'll be no shortage of office Machiavellians who will use whatever means at their disposal to get their way. And if you're in the way, prepare to be targeted. The key is to not let your guard down and to expect the worst from some people. If you get the plum project or the spacious office, this means that somebody else didn't. Unfortunately, jealousy has a regular place at the office table. Therefore, don't underestimate what some people will do to get what you have.

Take It with a Grain of Salt

You're sitting at your desk when the phone rings. It's your buddy in marketing with rumors that an audit has revealed serious discrepancies in your company's financial reporting. He thinks that the news could hit the business wires within an hour. Breathless, he begins speculating that both your jobs could be lost, along with everyone else's.

What do you do? First, don't panic. You cover as much ground as you can, calling on all your sources to get the real story. You sort out the facts. You take nothing for granted. In the end, you discover that the rumors, as is often the case, are greatly exaggerated. You save yourself a lot of grief in the process. In short, you're cool when others are not. This will reflect well on you.

The Power of the Personal

It's been said that the most potent currency in the workplace is the personal relationship. I agree. The development of good personal relationships helps you build the information pipeline that you're going to need to take your career to the next level. The key is treating everyone with whom you work with respect. That doesn't mean just the CEO but the mail-room attendant too. You might dismiss the notion of developing a friendly relationship with a secretary or an intern. Often these people are worth knowing because they're good people and because they're frequently gatekeepers to the real power players in your company. It's the right thing to do anyway, and the information you'll glean from these relationships will keep you plugged into office politics and give you an edge when the fur starts to fly.

Playing the Game

So how do you navigate the infighting, bruised egos, hurt feelings, back stabbing, and manipulation that flow through every workplace? Follow these rules and you'll earn a black belt in the art of office politics.

Get Your Act Together

Always be ready for an office power play directed against you. That means having records on file indicating correspondence you've had with coworkers and management on a project. E-mails are great because they provide dates and times—important evidence if you say that you told someone there was a problem on the Johnson account when you said you did. Compiling a paper trail is critical when somebody tries to roll you on a workplace issue. For example, suppose that your manager changed the deadline for the new product rollout, moving it back two weeks. You've got the memo to prove it. Sneaky Sam from sales says that you blew the deadline and cost the company some big business. You shove the deadline memo under Sneaky Sam's nose and delight as he stews in his own juices and the harsh spotlight turns on him. You gloat discreetly, of course.

Don't Give in to Gossip

Feel free to keep an ear open for good office information, but don't pass any along of your own. Occasionally, some good nuggets can be unearthed in the office rumor mill, information that you may be able to use to your advantage, such as the hush-hush but imminent opening for that position you've had your eye on.

Someone who gets a reputation as a gossip is someone who's not moving up the organization anytime soon. I can't say this enough—gossiping is a real career killer. Management won't take gossips seriously, and neither should you. Keep your ear to the ground—mix with the rank-and-file staff regularly to keep pace with their thoughts and feelings either about work or about their colleagues. Remember, nature gave us one tongue and two ears so that we could hear twice as much as we speak.

Read Between the Lines

Recognize that seemingly innocent questions from coworkers may be politically motivated. If someone asks you where you last worked or what your major was in college, she could be on a hunting expedition to find out whether you have the credentials to pull off the big account you've been assigned to pitch or handle the big engineering project. This person could be setting the stage for a power play that could result in you being removed from the account or being pulled from the big project. Be careful of tipping your hand and giving people too much information—some nefarious types could be plotting to use that information against you. This smacks of paranoia, but the less said to some people—particularly people you don't trust—the better.

Make a List

When you set out to influence a higher-up to give you what you want, make a list first. Suppose that you're in line to run a newly created department, a post that means more prestige, more pay, and more perks. You need to convince the CEO that you're the person for the job. Before you go in to talk to the big cheese, make a list of things you want to accomplish. What matters to this person? What information does the CEO need to give you the post. Is turf an issue? Ego? Budget? Find out what it takes to influence the big cheese and use it to your advantage.

Maintain a High Profile

Nobody wants to mess with someone who owns a high profile. Therefore, forge relationships with key company contacts and let it be known to these decision makers what you're up to. Copy them on e-mails and memos. Invite them to meetings. Build a case for yourself as a player to be taken seriously. Sometimes you may have to suck up to the brass by volunteering for their committees or task forces.

Be Ethical

Always act with class. Show respect for coworkers' opinions and goals (which is not necessarily the same thing as agreeing with them). Act in a trustworthy and honest fashion, even if others don't. Listen empathetically to your enemy's point of view and demonstrate that you understand it. Take your coworkers' objections seriously and consider them in a thoughtful and appropriate way. Show that you keep your word and do what you say.

Give Good Feedback

The key to giving—and even getting—feedback and making it useful is knowing how to give it and receive it tactfully. Always remember that when you take the initiative to give feedback to a colleague, you must do so carefully.

Don't Personalize Things

Suppose that you've decided to take the step to offer feedback to a colleague concerning a situation that has affected your work. Meet with the other person personally and briefly describe the situation from your point of view. Focus on describing the situation objectively and explain why it is hindering your performance. Try to limit the description of the problem and the feedback you are giving to a minute or less. Don't get involved with describing or criticizing personalities; the idea is to initiate dialogue.

Hear Others Out

Next, seek to understand your colleague's viewpoint. His or her perspective may be very different from yours. There may be extenuating circumstances guiding your colleague's actions. You may have to adjust your own view of the situation or, better yet, find ways to help your colleague contend with those extenuating issues.

Be Prepared to Compromise

Maybe you've heard the old adage that "half a loaf is better than none." This is especially true in the workplace, where you often have to give a little to get a lot. Suppose that you are trying to convince your public relations director to write a press release on your latest project, with quotes from you included. To get her sign-off, offer to help her back. Offer to write an article on the project for the corporate newsletter or take her out to lunch. She might think it over and say okay but that you'll have to write the release yourself and you can't be quoted (she wants the CEO for that). The end game here is to get the press release out, so take the deal and run.

Leave Your Options Open

Always leave people an out, especially you. Let's say that you've been assigned to a key company initiative to break into a new market.

Naturally, you're thrilled—until you hear that a troublesome coworker, Goofy Gus, has been assigned to work right alongside you. This loathsome creature isn't qualified to get out of bed in the morning and land on his feet. You weigh telling your boss that you object to the addition of Gus to the team. If you don't, your clueless coworker could botch the whole project with your name all over it. Best bet?

Explain your reservations to your boss. If she declines to replace Gus, you respond, "OK, I understand, and I hope you understand that I have to put my recommendations into writing. Look them over, and if you change your mind, let me know. Meanwhile, you have my word that I'll do my best to make this work." This step presents your boss with a problem of her own. If the project stumbles and your recommendation is in writing, your boss might have to explain why she didn't deep six Goofy Gus. But if she moves Gus to another position or project, this is good news, too. Either way, you both have options.

IGNORE OFFICE POLITICS AT YOUR OWN RISK

When it comes to office politics, it's play or be played. But if you're smart about it and keep a low profile (with your eyes and ears wide open), you can use office machinations and manipulations to great advantage.

Politically Savvy? Let's Find Out

Are you in the game or on the bench? How savvy are you to the effective use of office politics? Take this quick quiz to find out.

1. "You want something done? Ask a busy person," your boss says, handing you a file for a cost analysis that needs to be done. "Let me know when you can finish this." What do you do?

Continued

a. Call Fred in accounting, Bernice in computers, and Donna in word processing. Tell them that your boss is in a pinch and that he always remembers those who pitch in.

b. Stuff the file in your briefcase and work every night and weekend at home to get the analysis done.

c. Do the cost analysis, but only after you call your friend Susan in bookkeeping, meet her at the vending machines, and say, "My boss is the laziest. I heard that she has a one-way ticket out the front door!"

2. You have six days to produce a brochure for your accounting firm. You need to gather information, establish a distribution list, design the brochure, and write copy. Tomorrow you're supposed to be in Milwaukee for three days. What do you do?

a. Turn the job over to a vendor you know to be reliable, even though he isn't on your company's list of preferred vendors. If someone accuses you of ignoring the policy, say, "I didn't realize it was a problem. I was under a tight deadline and knew this vendor could get the job done."

b. Take the brochure file with you, write the copy in your motel room, and find a starving freelance designer in Milwaukee who'll work overtime.

c. Pore over the policies and procedures manual to find company-approved vendors. Then call Marge in word processing and complain, "Whoever selects our vendors has no design taste whatsoever!"

3. The loosey-goosey about George's department is that his number two manager plans to resign. This coveted position would be pivotal to your career. What will you do?

a. Hang out at the water cooler and keep your ears open. Plan a strategy, time, and place to talk to George. Position yourself as a viable candidate for the job.

b. Your good work and years with the company should speak for themselves. Expect to be noticed, and it will happen.

Continued

c. Tell everyone who'll listen that the job is an absolute nightmare so that they won't apply for it.

4. You've tried everything you can think of to get along with your boss. You've talked to him about work issues, asked others for advice, and attended training classes. Yet the relationship is as bad as ever. How can you win him over?

    a. Cut your losses and move on. You can't outlast a bad boss.

    b. Stay late and come in early. Make sure that he sees your full briefcase each night as you walk out.

    c. Become his source of all the office gossip. He will need to get along with you to hear what's on the grapevine.

5. You're the best technical writer in the department, yet you're consistently overlooked for promotion. What should you do?

    a. Showcase your talent areas besides technical writing. Seek a mentor who can help you move out of your seemingly dead-end position.

    b. Upgrade your image by changing your style of dress, placing a personal ad in the business section, and buying status office accessories.

    c. Make photocopies of your paycheck stub and distribute them to managers with a note: "Could you live on this?"

6. Your sales figures topped your quota by a record 21 percent last quarter, yet no one seems to be taking much notice. How will you go about getting the recognition you deserve?

    a. Keep a log of your new customers and submit a weekly report to your boss. Write an article for the business section of the newspaper on how to increase sales.

    b. Next quarter, reach 28 percent. You're sure to be noticed then.

    c. Post sales reports in the bathroom, the lunchroom, and on the bulletin board in the lobby. Share your news loudly with anyone who'll listen.

Continued

7. You and Don, who is a supervisor, have been working closely to land a national account. The two of you have been asked to present your proposed ad campaign at the account's headquarters in another city. Your relationship is strictly professional, but you're worried there'll be rumors if you travel together. What should you do?

   a. Be direct in telling coworkers that you're working with Don on the account. Tell them where you're going, where you'll be staying, and how to reach you.

   b. Thank Don for mentoring you, but tell him that you need to be seen working alone while you're in the office to avoid being the subject of office gossip.

   c. Hang out at the water cooler and start a juicy rumor about Don and the marketing vice president.

Scoring

To analyze your score, add up the number of *a*'s, *b*'s, and *c*'s. If you answered all *a*'s, you're an excellent team player who understands the finer points of office politics. You keep your eye on the goal—getting results—and you know how to tap not only your own strengths but also those of your coworkers.

If you chose mostly *b*'s, you're headed toward a permanent job as office martyr. By trying to do everything yourself, you'll work yourself into the ground and become bitter and resentful when you don't receive the recognition you deserve.

If you chose mostly *c*'s, people depend on you for gossip, not leadership. Everyone wants the inside scoop, but they rarely trust the person who's always dishing it out.

Source: *Working Woman's Communications Survival Guide*, by Ruth Herrman Siress, with Carolyn Riddle and Deborah Shouse. National Press Publications.

REALITY CHECK: AN AFFAIR NOT TO REMEMBER

Matt Stober found himself in a fine mess.

The 34-year-old manufacturing representative was caught in a vise: His boss was carrying on an affair with Stober's sales liaison, and nothing was getting done while the two carried on a torrid romance.

"I'm as open-minded as the next guy," Stober says. "But I don't think an office affair is a good idea in the first place—and especially when it affects my work performance."

Stober's dilemma was that his sales liaison wasn't that effective before she started carrying on with his employer. Now, acting under a perceived shield of cover due to her romance with Stober's boss, a company bigwig, she wasn't showing any signs of stepping up her performance.

"I was missing leads, not getting key phone messages, and receiving complaints from customers that their problems weren't being solved by our sales office," Stober recalls. "Those issues led directly to our sales liaison, who was our eyes and ears in the home office when we were out on the road selling."

Stober tried going to his boss and—keeping the romance out of it—said he needed better results from the sales office. Not taking the hint, the executive did little about it. Soon, though, the problem took care of itself when the sales liaison abruptly resigned from the company.

The bloom, it seemed, was finally off the rose. "Things got better after the liaison left, but I lost a lot of respect for my boss. I was glad when he was reassigned to the Kansas City office. Fifteen-hundred miles wasn't too far for me."

9

My Kingdom for a Yoda: Finding a Career Mentor

Luke had his Yoda. Frodo had his Gandalf. Elvis had his Colonel Parker. Even Ernie had his Burt.

They all needed a mentor to achieve great things. Chances are, you do too.

Having a wise old veteran in your corner—someone who advises you, looks out for your best interests, champions your career, and teaches you winning ways—isn't a luxury; it's a necessity. A good mentor can peel years off your career track.

What's a mentor? Think coach, guru, confident, advisor, and devil's advocate all rolled into one. Mentors have the experience, expertise, wisdom, and corporate cachet to teach, guide, counsel, and help a protégée to develop professionally and personally.

Mentors go back centuries. Alexander the Great got the inspiration he needed to conquer much of Europe and Asia from Homer, author of the *Odyssey* and the *Iliad*. He read these stories from an early age and imagined himself to be in the same line as the classic Greek heroes of yesteryear. Allegedly, Alexander the Great could recite large sections of the *Iliad* by heart. Historians also say that he had a special copy made for himself and took it with him on his exploits and conquests of two million square miles of the ancient world. Alexander the Great envisioned himself as Achilles, the great battlefield hero of Greek history whose accomplishments were recorded by Homer. In looking to emulate and outdo Achilles, Alexander the Great made Homer his mentor—someone he could turn to for inspiration and strength.

Alexander the Great didn't have a monopoly on the historical mentor thing. In Ben Franklin, Thomas Jefferson might have had the mentor of all mentors to turn to when he was writing the Declaration of Independence. Likewise, before General George Patton invaded and took Sicily from the Axis forces during World War II, he sought advice from the legendary U.S. General George Marshall.

Fast forward to the twenty-first century, where even Bill Gates has a mentor. His name is Warren Buffett, one of the greatest living stock market investors and, like Bill Gates, a multibillionaire. Gates often turns to his close friend Buffett for advice and counsel. Buffett is only too glad to give it.

If you see a slight pattern developing here, it's no accident. Throughout history, example after example shows that successful people often have turned to their wiser elders for help. This is especially true in the workplace today, where according to a survey by Leadership Development Consultants, Inc., almost 100 percent of female executives said that they had or have a mentor, and 65 percent of male executives said the same thing.

People who tap mentors for help recognize that they don't know everything and that there is strength in numbers. Thus they seek outside help from older, more experienced people whom they can trust. They don't turn to their neighbor in the next cubicle, whose main claim to fame is being able to recite every line from *Monty Python and the Holy Grail* or holding the company record for Nerf basketball. You want a pro here.

I had a mentor. I used to call on an old journalism professor of mine from time to time and more frequently as both of us grew accustomed to each other. He'd given me my first reference out of college and had told me his door was always open. I don't know that he saw anything special in me—like the college professor who guided Mitch Albom in his best-seller *Tuesdays with Morrie*. However, I saw something special in him and was glad for the help. In fact, when I think back on it, I can't imagine not having had someone I could call on for advice when things got hurly-burly in a hurry.

My mentor was great at providing career direction without actually giving me the right answers. This was intentional on his part. The answers I would have to glean for myself. However, my mentor always set me on the right path so that the answers were right in front of me. His only request of me was that I open a door or two for a protégée of my own someday, a task I look forward to.

QUALITIES OF A MENTOR

Having had a good mentor of my own and having talked to many other people who have shared a similar experience, here are the attributes I think matter most in a mentor:

- *Someone who has respect and is respected.* You want someone who has the dignity to treat other people right. You also want someone with clout and connections and who knows how to use them.

- *Someone who believes in you.* Your mentor should champion you in the workplace with good reason—because you possess the qualities that are critical to succeeding professionally. A mentor who has doubts about you is as useful as a gutter on the *Titanic*.

- *Someone who is a positive thinker.* Most people respond to optimists better than they do to pessimists. You don't want a mentor who sugarcoats everything, but you do want one who sees the best in people and can get the best out of you.

- *Someone who holds you accountable.* There's no need for a wishy-washy mentor. If he or she gives you advice that you don't act on or dismiss outright, then it might be time for your mentor to get in your face about it. You're in this together, and your mentor should hold your feet to the fire when you screw up (and you will—it's called a learning experience).

- *Someone who is accessible.* Ideally, it's best if you can see your mentor on a regular basis, face to face if possible. E-mail and phone calls will suffice. Letters are fine, too. What you don't want is a mentor who's never around to do any major-league mentoring.

- *Someone who is discreet.* Everything you say to your mentor should be kept in the strictest confidence. Good mentors are already adept at keeping secrets; otherwise, they never would have hit it big on their own. But a mentor who can't keep your most private career thoughts in confidence can't be trusted at all.

TIPS ON FINDING A MENTOR

Finding a mentor isn't easy. Often it can be downright scary. It's not easy to ask someone for the kind of career help you need. Some people say "No." Frequently, though, the question never needs to be asked—mentorships just happen. There's no clergyman up there on the altar pronouncing you "mentor" and "protégée." You may go through a 20-year mentor-type relationship where the word *mentor* never comes up. You may go through trial-and-error periods where you don't feel comfortable with a mentor you've chosen. Having said this, when you do begin actively seeking a mentor, the following rules should make your search easier.

Begin Early

The earlier you find a good mentor, the better. Remember, the whole point of a mentor relationship is to shave years off your career track. Starting early, therefore, even before your first professional job, is highly advisable.

If you can make a connection from college or even high school, this is great. If not, try joining your local Chamber of Commerce, many of which are stocked with experienced business types who won't mind lending a young up-and-comer like you a helping hand.

If you grow close to a boss at work and are transferred to another department or move to another company, don't hesitate to cash in on that good relationship and forge some mentorship ties. Wise to the ways of the business world, your old boss won't hesitate to say, "Gee, I wouldn't do that, and here's why," or "Try this approach and see if it doesn't produce better results for you." Your old boss knows you and he knows business—good credentials for any career mentor.

Are You Experienced?

In virtually every case, your mentor will be older than you. Also, he or she won't be your boss. Your mentor could be an old college professor, an old boss, a parent (sometimes—but it's hard for Mom or Dad to be objective), an older family member (such as a sister or an uncle), or someone you simply look up to and with whom you enjoy a good relationship. It is perfectly normal for mentorships to develop between junior- and senior-level employees at the same company. Some companies, in fact, encourage mentorships, with official programs of their own to match younger workers with older ones.

Consider a Pro

Sometimes you just can't find a mentor you like or, worse, can trust. If this is the case, consider a professional mentor. Professional mentors include executive coaches, trainers, therapists, and consultants, and you should expect a good match between your needs and their abilities. The relationship will be on a financial basis, and you can make more specific or exacting demands on such a mentor. This may be most appropriate for mentor relationships with a clearly defined time span, for example, to support you during the early stages of a new job or to pass a specific examination.

Take Control

If you work for an employer who has a formal mentoring program, take advantage of it. Some companies will offer financial incentives to executives who offer their time as mentors. You also should attend trade shows and industry breakfasts and luncheons and, most important, strike up conversations with seasoned professionals wherever you go. Don't feel that you have to stick with people in your industry—sometimes the best advice and knowledge can be gleaned from outside your specialty area.

Look for Certain Qualities

You want a mentor who demonstrates good judgment so that he or she can help you understand the consequences of your decisions. You want someone who is street smart as well as book smart. People who lack street smarts often get rolled in the rough-and-tumble world of office politics. Having someone who has survived, even thrived, in the gritty side of the business and who can pass along some timely tips is a big advantage for you. You want someone who doesn't give up, too. Resiliency is a wonderful trait for an executive, but not everyone knows how to keep slugging away when the odds are stacked against them.

No Bossa Nova

By and large, your boss should not be your mentor. He or she has enough responsibility getting your department running like a Swiss watch. Besides, someone who handles your annual evaluation and provides raises and promotions shouldn't mentor you. Your coworkers will balk, and rightly so. A good boss won't take a mentorship role with you anyway, because he or she already has a supervisory role. What's good for your company and what's good for you aren't necessarily the same thing. This doesn't mean that your mentor shouldn't be an insider at your workplace. An ex-boss or older coworker who knows the local terrain is of great value to you. Some organizations keep lists of people who have volunteered to serve as mentors, and you could select someone from the list. If your workplace doesn't keep a list and you haven't met anyone who you think would make a good mentor, ask for suggestions from your colleagues in the human resources, staff development, or education departments.

Be Realistic

When you're looking for a mentor, don't expect a miracle worker who'll have you swilling champagne in the executive dining room within six months. Your expectations should be grounded when going the mentor route. Look for someone who can provide perspective and won't lie to you. This is a good mentor-in-the-making.

A mentor such as this will be there to candidly answer such questions as, "What is the informal organization of this company?" "What does it take to be promoted here?" or "What type of volunteer or committee work is valued by this institution?" And when you get ideas of your own, your mentor should be a solid sounding board, ready to listen patiently and provide feedback that you may not want to hear.

Stick with a Success Story

The best mentors are the people who have ridden out the bumps in their own careers, have learned from them, and have succeeded in their own careers as a result. Ideally, therefore, you want someone with stellar career navigation skills. Having said this, there is no reason that you can't have a mentor from the outside world too. An old football coach or a homeless shelter director you met volunteering in your community can also be successful mentors. For that matter, there's no reason you can't have multiple mentors. For instance, you can have a mentor at your company to guide you through your career challenges and a mentor in your private life to lead you by example and show you how to become a complete person. (By the way, volunteering for community projects will give you visibility and a reputation as a team player—someone others will want to help out.)

Ask Your Company for Help

If you can't find a mentor on your own, ask your firm for some guidance. The human resources (HR) department is a good place to start—HR personnel know everyone at the company and are in the business of helping employees anyway. Your boss could come in handy, too. Ask if he or she knows of anyone who can help you succeed in the company. Like your HR director, your boss knows many people in the company, especially at the management level, and should be able to help you out. Any approach that makes you a more productive and happy employee should be okay with your boss.

At Miami-based Knight Ridder, Inc., the company has implemented a program called Project Bench Strength. The program, which is managed at the corporate level, involves a handful of senior executives working with a select, diverse group of field employees who possess leadership potential, for example, a technical professional whose next step could be information systems director.

Make a List

Mentors respond well to protégées who ask the right questions—about themselves and about their mentors. Before you focus on a mentor, ask yourself

- What skills do I need in order to get where I want to go?
- Which skills need fine-tuning?
- What do I want from a mentorship?

When you zero in on a potential mentor, study your relationship with this person and try to draw some conclusions:

- Does this person have a direct and thorough understanding of my work, my stage in life, and me?
- Is this person senior to me in work experience or stage of life?
- Is this person willing to be my mentor?
- Do I respect this person and want to be more like him or her?
- Does this person inspire me to do and be my best?
- Is this person trustworthy?
- Is this person genuinely interested in me—or looking for something in return?
- Does this person see potential in me and encourage its development?
- Might this person see himself or herself reflected in me?
- Is this person good at seeing the big picture?
- How much time will this person give to mentoring?
- How accessible is this person?
- Can I take problems to this person without feeling embarrassed, defensive, or defeated?
- Above all, does this person believe in me?

CLOSE THE LOOP

Here are some more hands-on tips for finding a mentor:

- Contact industry trade organizations. A professional trade organization already may have a scheme to help identify mentors or may offer assistance via a newsletter, Web site, etc. However, beware of being offered someone with the necessary time but whose experience or skills are out of date.

- Contact local businesses or organizations. Organizations such as the Chamber of Commerce may be able to help find a mentor for you. Local businesses or organizations may be able to provide you with the names of retired executives who may be willing to act as volunteer mentors. I did something similar and found a retired financial advisor who became one of my best sources for stories when I was freelancing for Dow Jones, CBS News, and some other media outlets. After a while, I discovered that we weren't really talking about Wall Street or any other topic relating to a story I was covering. We were talking about life and what makes us happy. I had just gotten married, my wife was pregnant with our first child, and I was apprehensive about providing for a family as a freelance writer. My mentor convinced me that doing what I loved not only would bring home the bacon but also would make me a better husband and father too. My retired friend passed away suddenly a few days after I had spoken to him, and I felt an emptiness in my life for a long time afterward. Just a great guy.

- If you are enrolled in a college or university, make an appointment with student career services to find out if they have a list of volunteer mentors.

- Enroll in a college or university extension course to gain access to faculty members who could be potential mentors.

- Get on the Internet and research trade publications associated with your industry and identify potential mentors from the biographic or topical articles. Then e-mail the publications and ask whether they have personnel who can act as mentors.

- Connect with exhibit areas of conferences and conventions associated with your field; these are often free-admission events staffed by experienced persons who could be potential mentors. If you are lucky enough to attend industry trade shows on behalf of your company, network like crazy when you get there. Bring business cards and hand them out like candy. Not only are you planting the seeds for good mentorships, but you also are raising your profile in the industry.

- Ask your friends and relatives to keep alert to someone who could help you. After all, they know you best.

- Visit a retirement or senior citizen center and let the staff know that you are looking for a mentor in a certain area.

- Just like Alexander the Great did with Homer and Achilles, read biographies of people who have been greats in your field; sometimes the biography itself can act as a mentor.

GENDER AND MENTORS

One last thing on mentors: There's no rulebook on mentors. There's no blueprint, formula, or cookie-cutter approach to finding a mentor who is right for you and your career.

It's hardly a secret, however, that some potential protégées may have a strong preference for a mentor of the same sex.

Gender and mentorships are tough issues and often a tough mix. Do you really want to wade into a personal relationship with a mentor of the opposite sex? Some people are strong enough to handle this, and some aren't.

In addition, reducing the pool of mentor candidates by half cuts your mentorship options dramatically.

The good news is that gender may not be as important as we assume. Research in the United States shows that protégées rarely report gender as an issue in a successful mentoring relationship.

Obviously, there are cases where gender is an issue. Thus, if you do enter into a protégée-mentor relationship, keep these issues in mind:

- *Establish a code of contact.* Nothing too heavy-handed, mind you. Just lay out some ground rules about where you'll meet and when. Talk about what ground you want to cover. Above all, keep things open and aboveboard. After all, there may be spouses and partners involved. People could get hurt easily if you fall head over heels for a power figure (which is what mentors are to most protégées).

- *Fight patronization.* Not to stereotype here, but some older men have a habit of overprotecting younger women, even to the point of keeping the truth from them. This is patronizing, plain and simple. Tell your mentor that you don't want to be protected—you want to be led.

- *Know what different mentors bring to the table.* Like a mother or father, many mentors are stronger in some areas and weaker in others. Male mentors may be more adept at office politics, especially the importance of schmoozing and socializing in climbing the career ladder. Female mentors are more likely to teach their protégées by sharing their own experiences in solving problems, according to a recent study from Pennsylvania

State University's School of Graduate Professional Studies.*
They are also more likely to impart the people skills that it
takes to work effectively in the flattened organizational structure many companies are adopting.

Traditionally, companies often have shied away from allowing
senior workers to mentor younger protégées of the opposite sex.
However, the Penn State study shows that men can provide needed
career assistance to younger workers and that women mentors can
provide the nurturing and social skills that team-oriented organizations demand.

- Male mentors were perceived to give their protégées more
  support in career development than female mentors.
- Female mentors were perceived to provide more acceptance,
  coaching, and counseling and to serve as role models more
  than male mentors.
- Protégées perceived women mentors to be better role models, that is, to provide behaviors that the protégées could identify with.
- Protégées also trusted and had more respect for their female
  mentors, whom they perceived to hold higher standards than
  men.
- Female protégées valued the career development provided by
  their male mentors more than males, perhaps because of the
  so-called glass ceiling.

*John J. Sosik and Veronica M. Godshalk, "The Role of Gender in Mentoring: Implications
for Diversified and Homogenous Mentoring Relationships." Pennsylvania State
University, Great Valley School of Graduate Professional Studies, Department of
Management, 1999.

Resources for Finding a Mentor

Mentoring services on the Internet:

- Find a Mentor. This organization maintains a database of mentors and has a matching service. It has a free and a fee-based service, and it also provides booklets on mentoring as well as a product reward system for paid members.
- Mentor Program Listings. Many universities and organizations provide mentors for their students or community members. Check out this list to see if your university or organization is there.
- Just Plain Mentors. This is an organization and system that specializes in providing mentors who are associated with various show business professions.
- MentorU.com. A virtual mentoring community. Individuals can sign up for mentoring from some of the leading experts and authors in motivation, business, and goal achievement. The focus of the mentoring can be on personal growth, business development, technology, sales and marketing, making presentations, leadership, or communications.
- America's Promise. This is part of a national campaign in the United States to connect youth and mentors.
- Volunteers of America. This is an organization with a long history of providing mentors.
- Youth Service America. This organization is focused on helping young people help others in their communities.
- National Council of Volunteer Centers. This is a good way to find local resources in communities around the United States.
- Advoco. This organization connects individuals seeking advice with expert advisors across a range of categories (fees are sometimes required).
- Advisor.com. This is a complete advice system for persons involved in e-commerce and interested in growing an Internet business. *Continued*

- Ask the Employer.com. This is an innovative e-mentoring career advancement site where registrants can search for an online mentor or sign up to become a professional mentor. In addition, this site offers career advice, job-hunting tips, and small business information. It is free of charge to search for a mentor or register to become a mentor.

- San Francisco Woman-to-Woman Peer Mentoring Program. This organization helps women get connected to other women who can teach what women want to learn.

- Reach4it. This is a free service that connects mentors with youth and others and includes forms for people to sign up as either mentors or partners.

- Razzberry. This is a service that specializes in helping women and girls find mentors and be mentors to others.

- MentorNet. This is a service, typically for university-level persons, to connect women interested in science, technology, and engineering with mentors.

- Prime Stage. This is a professional theater organization that provides one-on-one mentors for writers, designers, graphic artists, and technical personnel.

- Sponsors for Educational Opportunity (SEO) Career Program. This program provides young people (from middle schools through colleges) of color with opportunities to gain work experience in top-level corporations in the New York metropolitan area. When a young person is accepted into the program, he or she is matched with an alumni mentor (from previous SEO placements) and a mentor from within his or her work placement.

- Virtual Volunteering Project. This is a large listing of e-mail mentoring and tutoring resources and connections that can be used for either becoming a mentor or finding a mentor or tutor who uses e-mail as the primary means of contact.

Continued

- Xavier University Alumni Find-a-Mentor Service. Students and graduates of Xavier University can register and use this alumni service to find a mentor in a variety of fields. (For additional university find-a-mentor services, visit the mentor program descriptions.)
- California State University at Northridge. This is a service provided for students at CSUN by alumni. (For additional university find-a-mentor services, visit the mentor program descriptions.)

REALITY CHECK: MIND OVER MENTOR: NOT FOR THIS PROMISING EXECUTIVE

A mentor doesn't have to be in the same office, the same company—even the same area code.

For Kim Hawes, 29-year-old financial analyst for a burgeoning Philadelphia-based exercise equipment manufacturer, a mentoring relationship occurred long-distance with her old economics professor at Colorado State.

"I had taken the position in Philly and worked there for about four years before I hit the wall, so to speak," recalls Hawes, an exercise buff in her own right. "I wasn't getting promoted and wasn't meeting my career goals. Here I was turning 30 soon, and I wasn't happy with my career."

During a long weekend in Fort Collins, Colorado, at a friend's wedding, Hawes literally bumped into her old professor at the reception. "She turned out to be a friend of the bride's family, too," says Hawes. "We talked all evening and had a great time."

When her old professor gave Hawes her card and told her to call or e-mail any time, the aspiring executive took it to heart and called within a week, asking for advice on how to get her career back on track. A series of e-mails and phone calls followed over the ensuing months, with the professor requesting a "career outline" from Hawes that would give the professor a better picture of where Hawes was and where she wanted to be career-wise.

"She told me that my current company wasn't a great fit for me, as they weren't promoting a lot of females to executive positions," Hawes says. "I bided my time, began looking around, and found a senior financial analyst position with a health foods company that month. More money, better title—it all worked out great. Just because I bumped into an old college professor at a wedding."

10

Belching Your Career Goodbye: The Fine Art of Business Etiquette

What do you make of the following scenarios?

- You're at a business luncheon with your boss and three big clients. You hold up the order because you can't decide what you want to eat. *Result:* A big career downer. People who can't decide between the stromboli or the chicken Kiev in front of the boss send a message that they are indecisive, annoying, and maybe even a bit rude.

- You're traveling with your boss and some coworkers to a big convention. Many of your company's clients will be there too. The airplane ascends, and after a while, you decide to take a snooze. You pop the release button and recline your seat to the max. Little do you know that a top client is sitting right behind you and you've reclined your seat just as she's about to take a forkful of applesauce. As the tray digs into her belly, her fork misses its mark and instead veers into her eye. Applesauce is everywhere. *Result:* You don't pay an immediate price, aside from a surly look from the offended party. Later in the week, however, the client walks up to your company's booth at the convention. Recognizing you as the rude recliner from flight 438, she pulls $50,000 worth of business to teach your firm a lesson.

- You show up for work after a big night out on the town. Your clothes are wrinkled, you're hung over, and you smell like a brewery. *Result:* Showing up for work in such a condition tells management that you have no respect for the company and the people who work for it.

A professional who is guilty of these infractions is in serious need of a lesson in business etiquette. Lack of basic business etiquette skills can be a real career killer. People want to associate with and be led by professionals who exude class and dignity and have a deep reservoir of consideration and respect for others. In short, they want people with good etiquette skills.

How do you know if you need to spruce up on your business manners? Here are a few keys:

- If your idea of etiquette is not cutting in front of the guy in front of you at the big keg party, you might be short on business etiquette.

- If you order the duck l'orange at a business meal and proceed to eat it with your hands, you might be short on business etiquette.

- If you're one of those people who likes to type your e-mails in capital letters, you might be short on business etiquette.

- If you leave phone calls unreturned and e-mails unanswered, you might be short on business etiquette.

- If you travel a lot and insist on packing a steamer trunk full of your stuff for the trip, you might be short on business etiquette (and nobody will want to travel with you).

- If you have a handshake so weak that it gives your grandmother the heebie-jeebies, you might be short on business etiquette.

- If you interrupt people at meetings, on conference calls, and on the phone, you might be short on business etiquette.

- If you dress like you're going to appear on *The Jerry Springer Show* instead of at a job interview, you might be short on business etiquette.

- If you consider personal hygiene to be an overrated character trait, you might be short on business etiquette, although not on flies.

- If you preface every remark you make to your coworkers, managers, and clients with an obscenity or two, you might be short on business etiquette.

THE DEVIL'S IN THE DETAILS

There's a wonderful saying from Proverbs 15:23,28: "How wonderful it is to say the right thing at the right time. A good man thinks before he speaks; the evil man pours out his evil words without a thought."

Loosely translated, this means that what you don't know about business etiquette can kill your career. Whether it's knowing which one's the bread plate or what time to arrive for a job interview, the subtle nuances of business etiquette can distinguish and elevate you from the lumbering clods and ham-handed oafs who don't bother boning up on the business niceties.

Why the big deal over a salad fork or a handshake? Because if you can't conduct yourself professionally in business and social situations, people assume, fairly or not, that you lack the care and self-control necessary to be executive material. Etiquette means presenting yourself in a way that shows that you mean to be taken seriously. It also means making people comfortable around you—and you around them.

With business etiquette, you increase your visibility and respect around the workplace. People will remember that you sent a condolence card after the death of a loved one or helped the interns clean up the conference room after a business lunch. They'll notice that you're the first one to greet a new staffer or say "please" and "thank you" not just to the chief executive officer (CEO) but also to the cleaning staff.

Let's face facts. Given the option of promoting the guy who literally licks his plate clean at a client dinner and addresses the waiter as "Hey, you" or the person who conducts himself with class and is a pleasant conversationalist during the meal, who would you choose if you owned the business? If you want to stay in business long, you'll take your chances with the employee who can handle himself in public and make your company look good doing so.

TIPS ON OFFICE ETIQUETTE

There's no shortage of gaffes and blunders awaiting the career professional unwise in the ways of business etiquette. Here are some dos and don'ts of office etiquette. Do . . .

Wait to be invited into someone's office or cubicle. No, I don't mean a written invitation. But barging into someone's workspace without consent is a sign that the offender has no respect for the other person's privacy. A simple knock on the door or a quick call ahead of time should do the trick.

Avoid using the speakerphone. Unless you're fortunate enough to have an office and can close the door, don't pump up the volume and share your phone calls with your coworkers. I don't know what it is about speakerphone conversations, but they seem to encourage both participants to converse at a decibel more appropriate for an AC/DC concert or a Bears-Packers football game. If you like to roam around with your hands free while you talk on the phone, get a nice headset and save everyone a lot of grief.

Handle cell phone calls delicately. Suppose that you're in a coworker's cubicle discussing the specs on the Mortimer account and your cell phone rings (or beeps, chirps, or plays the opening stanza of "Mack the Knife"). You've got a decision to make here. Do you whip out the phone and give a condescending "Hush" to your coworker as you take the call? Or do you excuse yourself and walk away from the cubicle to answer the phone? You could avoid both options and let the phone ring for a while before it goes into voice mail. But the time it takes for that to happen leads to awkwardness while you wait for the phone to go quiet. Better to excuse yourself if you have to take the call. Better yet, leave the phone in your workspace. A meeting's a meeting whether it's in the conference room or an associate's cubicle.

Speak quietly. If there's one thing that will drive your coworkers screaming yellow bonkers, it's having to listen to the office "foghorn" all day. All workplaces are different, but the one thing they all have in common is that people gather there to work—not to provide an audience for "Megaphone Mary" from accounting or "Surround-Sound Sam" from sales. Treat your office like a library and leave the foghorn at home.

Schedule meetings ahead of time and manage them appropriately. Let participants know beforehand what the agenda will be. Tell them what the objective will be too. Also include the expected duration of the meeting. By and large, try to keep meetings short. Make sure that you thank everyone for attending, and keep the meeting on track. If troublemakers insist on deviating from the agenda, tell them that you'll be glad to take the item "offline" for a private discussion later. When the meeting's finished, have the minutes written up so that people can see how they contributed—or not.

Make proper introductions. The best way to make an introduction is to introduce a lower-ranking person to a higher-ranking person. For example, if your CEO is Ms. Howell and you are introducing administrative assistant Karen Jones to her, the correct introduction would be, "Ms. Howell, I'd like you to meet Karen Jones." If you forget a person's name while making an introduction, don't panic. Proceed with the introduction with a statement such as, "I'm sorry, your name has just slipped my mind." Omitting an introduction is a bigger faux pas than salvaging a botched introduction. Also, always stand up when being introduced to someone. If you find yourself sitting across a large table, it may not be possible to reach across and shake hands. But stand anyway—it's a sign of respect.

Extend a firm handshake. The physical connection you make when shaking hands with someone can leave a powerful impression. When someone's handshake resembles a warm, wet mackerel, people will notice. A firm handshake made with direct eye contact sets the stage for a positive encounter. Remember, whether you're a man or a woman, jobs can still be won or lost on the basis of a firm handshake. Men and women should shake hands with each other the same way as woman-to-woman or man-to-man. Offer your hand turned at a 90-degree angle to the floor, and don't hold just the fingers or try to crush the other person's hand with a Vulcan death grip you saw on *Star Trek.* A tip: During a cocktail hour, hold your drink in the left hand. Do this both to keep your right hand free and to prevent it from being cold and wet from holding a glass. If you're a lefty, just switch the glass into your right hand.

Don't . . .

Interrupt people. Listening is a lost art in business, but CEO after CEO says that a big reason that he or she grabbed the brass ring was because they were good listeners. This is great advice for a young up-and-comer. If you are listening, this means that you are also paying attention. If you're not, this usually means that you're wasting time and accomplishing nothing. Thus, if you're in a face-to-face meeting or in a group of people discussing a workplace issue, don't feel obligated to pipe in for the sake of it. If you have a vocal contribution to make, wait for a good opening and speak up. But don't interrupt someone who's speaking and usurp that person's time. Your coworkers will resent it. If you have to interrupt—or you just want to excuse yourself and get away from what you consider to be a pointless conversation—apologize and leave with a promise that you'll talk again later.

Be conversationally challenged. I've already discussed the art of schmoozing and how it can increase your workplace visibility and help you get ahead in your career. Making conversation is basically the same idea. The key is to remember to maintain eye contact and not to interrupt people. It's worth your while to keep apprised of major news events so that you can contribute value to the conversation. Be discreet about what you discuss in a business conversation, especially with a new client or new manager or coworker. No talking about your health or your sex life or engaging in gossip or back stabbing. Also, do not correct someone's grammar. Nobody likes a know-it-all.

Show up at a convention or other big-time networking event without name tags and business cards. When wearing a name tag, put it on your right side, up toward the shoulder. This is the easiest viewing position for the person you are meeting. Why? Because when you shake hands, the other person's eyes are already going in that direction. Your business cards also are critical for business contacts. If you don't carry them, some people might get the impression that you don't care about your job or your company.

Don't make an office visitor wait for more than 15 minutes after your appointed meeting time. Everybody's busy, and nobody will fault you for being a few minutes late. But when the clock goes beyond 15 minutes or so, your visitor may start to wonder how important he is to you. When your visitor is called into your office or cubicle, stand to greet him and put aside anything else you are doing. Even if you are on the phone, excuse yourself as soon as possible. Make your visitor think, at that moment, that he is the most important person in the world to you.

TIPS FOR DRESSING RIGHT ON THE JOB

One of the worst mistakes otherwise decent employees make on the job is in choosing what they wear to work in the morning.

Sure, dressing down is a business trend, but this doesn't mean that you should clothe yourself like you're gunning for the assistant manager slot at the Quickie Mart or a walk-on role in Tim Burton's next Gothic flick.

Understandably, business dress codes these days can be confusing. Few people are dead-solid certain about what constitutes "casual" wear. Some overcompensate by wearing shirts and ties (for guys) and skirts and blouses (for women). Some undercompensate by wearing sandals, dirty T-shirts, ripped jeans, and nose rings. I'm as open minded as the next person, but I've yet to meet a CEO with a nose ring.

Thus you must dress like a professional to be considered a professional. One study says that up to 95 percent of the time employees are judged for such things as hiring or promotion in the first two to three minutes of visual contact. Clothing allows you to make an excellent case for yourself as management material. If your clothing is attractive and well coordinated, you feel more confident, and this is reflected in your behavior. On the other hand, if your clothes are unattractive or not well coordinated, you may withdraw, evoking a negative reaction from your coworkers, clients, and management.

Here are some pointers on the business dress code:

- Ill-fitting clothing is never acceptable. Whether this means a suit that is too tight or a skirt that needs alteration. With more casual dressing, fit is extremely important to the professionalism of the look. Unfortunately, the attitude that often accompanies wearing more casual clothing is less attention to fit. Take a critical look at the clothes you are wearing to work. Are they too baggy? Too tight?

- Examine your wardrobe critically each season. Older shirts or pants that have been dry cleaned so many times that they're shiny should be given away, donated to a worthy charity, or relegated to weekend wear—just as long as you remove them from your work wardrobe. Clothing, even clothing that was expensive and of high quality when purchased, can just get worn out and lose its sharp, professional look.

- The following are some no-no's for business dress: shorts, jeans (except for special occasions), festive printed shirts, T-shirts of any kind, tank tops, sneakers, topsiders, walking shoes, or athletic shoes.

- Typically, business dress for men means a dark gray or navy blue wool suit; a long-sleeved, all-cotton shirt; a silk necktie (no outrageous prints); plain, dark lace-up or slip-on shoes; high, dark socks that won't slide down; and no jewelry other than a watch, cuff links, and a wedding band.

- Women's clothing is a bit more complicated because there's a wider range of clothing options to choose from. Generally, though, women should choose a knee-length or longer suit or dress with long sleeves in a natural fabric, closed-toe pumps, and a briefcase or purse. Women should avoid tight or revealing clothes and excessive jewelry. Always wear stockings, even in summer.

- Not all companies require traditional business dress, but few interviewers will fault you for dressing formally. If you're afraid that you'll make a negative impression in business dress, pay a discreet visit to the company to get an idea of what the employees wear. Be sure to visit in the middle of the week so that a "casual" Monday or Friday dress code doesn't throw you off. One caveat: The engineering department may have a different standard of dress from, say, the sales department, so don't assume that just because some employees are wearing jeans, you should too.

- A basic wardrobe that meets the needs of most career professionals includes 2 suits, 2 jackets or blazers, 3 pairs of trousers (for men), 3 skirts (for women), and 10 shirts or blouses. Compare the items you already own with this list. If there is a great difference between what you already have and what you need, don't try to buy everything at once. It often takes years to build a classic, effective wardrobe. If you don't have a hefty salary and can't afford much, don't worry about it. A few good-quality clothes are better than a closet full of low-quality duds.

A Word on Formal Wear

As you rise in the executive ranks, you'll find your social calendar filling with dinners, cocktail parties, banquets, and charitable events. Before you "quoth" like the raven and say, "Nevermore," because you don't know what to wear, think again. Here's a rundown on the social wear set:

White tie. This is the term used to mean more formal garments that include a black tailcoat with matching trousers trimmed by two lines of braid on the outside of each trouser leg, a white tie, white single- or double-breasted vest, or a wing-collar shirt with a stiff front. Special shoes are required, generally a patent leather pump. On some occasions, white gloves are used, and more infrequently, a top hat is worn. This white tie attire usually is limited to very formal occasions, such as a wedding or a presidential inaugural, and even then it is only worn by the principals.

Black tie. Generally, most black tie events will be noted as such on the invitation. Black tie dress consists of the following: black tuxedo coat and trousers, tux shirt with straight or winged collar, tux bow tie, and matching waist cummerbund. (Formal dressing demands that the waistband of the trouser never be exposed.) Black shoes and tux (silk or polish cotton) socks are a must. Tux braces can be worn to help trousers to fit properly. For seasonal, festival, or tropical formal events, a colored tux coat can be worn. For example, the white tux dinner jacket with regular black tux trousers is popular for the right event during the spring and summer or on a cruise. Other colored dinner jackets can be worn depending strictly on the occasion. Colored coat and trouser tuxes are not acceptable except in very unusual situations.

Semiformal. This generally means that a tuxedo is not required and that a dressy suit would be appropriate. For example, a solid dark navy blue suit with a white French cuff shirt would be acceptable.

One benefit of going to a quality specialty clothing store is that the person selling the clothing will have the background and understanding to give you good direction and advice on dressing for every occasion.

TIPS ON BUSINESS MEAL ETIQUETTE

We all have a little Emily Post in us dying to get out. The trouble is that she's usually outweighed by the Mo, Larry, and Curly in us trying to stuff her back inside.

Fortunately, watching your P's and Q's at a business meal isn't too complicated as long as you remember a few rules.

The Place Setting

The general principle is to work from the outside in. For example, salad comes first, so you start with the fork on the far left. With each course, simply use the next utensil in line; the utensils closest to your plate are for the last course. One major exception: You'll find your dessert spoon above your plate, perpendicular to the other utensils. The waiters will pour water and other beverages in the appropriate glass for you, so you won't have to figure out which goblet to use; just drink out of the one that's full. When you're finished eating, cross the utensils neatly over your plate to signal the waiter that you're done. Most important, don't let silverware overwhelm you—servers are there to provide extras if you need them. Using a salad fork with your steak isn't ideal, but it also isn't a deal breaker.

Sitting Down

Think fast. Your napkin should go into your lap within the first 10 seconds of sitting down. Once in your lap, the napkin should remain off the table until everyone leaves at the end of the meal. If you need to stand or leave the table during the meal, the napkin should be left on your chair. In fancy settings, servers will serve from the right and clear from the left. Lean accordingly.

Table Conduct

Which will it be, Fred Astaire or Fred Flintstone? The answer could have a major impact on your career. If you're Fred Astaire, you chew with your mouth closed, keep your elbows off the table, and don't talk with your mouth full. A tip: Take small bites. Anything you need to remove from your mouth should come out the way it came in— if you are eating your fish with a fork, take out the bones with a fork—as discretely as possible. If you wonder how your own table manners look to others, here's another tip: The next time you eat at home, put a mirror on the table or set up the camcorder and watch yourself eat. This is what your client sees. A few more things: Abstain from alcohol. Hey, I like a few beers now and then, but there's a time and a place for it. And a business meal isn't the time or place. Acting like a top candidate for The Betty Ford Center will penalize you severely career-wise. Also, turn off your cell phone during a client lunch, or at least warn your dining companions that you are expecting a particular call. When you are finished with your meal, place your fork upside down on the plate and put your folded napkin on the bread plate.

Who's Got the Tab?

Don't start a fight over the bill—it would be a pity to make it through the meal and lose a job or an account because you couldn't agree on who was covering the tab. If you've invited a business associate to dinner, it's your bill to pay. To avoid any scenes, arrive at the restaurant a few minutes early, tell your server that you are entertaining a client, and ask him or her to run your credit card through. Then the bill will come straight to you, and all you have to do at the end of the meal is figure the tip and sign your name.

When the check arrives, don't reach for it. If a company representative has invited you to a business meal in hopes of recruiting you, the tab is on him or her.

Top 10 Business Dining Mistakes

According to Perrin Cunningham, owner of In Good Company, Inc., and a Los Gatos, California-based business etiquette trainer, the top 10 table manner mistakes are as follows:

1. Chewing or talking with your mouth open
2. Burping
3. Picking your teeth
4. Piling purses, keys, eyeglasses, etc. on the table
5. Leaving your cell phone on (Keep it off or on vibrate.)
6. Poor posture—slouching, hunching, or reclining
7. Eating too fast or slow for the group's pace
8. Holding silverware and gesturing like you are conducting an orchestra
9. Smoking or chewing gum
10. Shouting, whispering, or otherwise disturbing other diners

A Table Manners Snapshot

- No elbows on the table, please.

- Chew with your mouth closed.

- Hold the silverware correctly.

- Pass food to the right.

- Pass both the salt and the pepper.

- Butter hot bread by opening bread with fork and butter it all.

- Break hot or cold bread and eat it one bite at a time.

- Keep your feet flat on the floor.

- Sit up straight in your chair.

- Modify your voice so that you are talking short range.

- Excuse yourself to people on each side if you should leave the table.

- If you have to refuse anything, simply say, "No thank you." No explanation is necessary.

- Pass the butter with the butter knife on the dish.

- When stirring and seasoning iced tea, drop the lemon into the glass, pierce it with a spoon, and quietly move the spoon up and down in the glass.

- "Please pass the _____." or "May I have the _____?" is the correct way to ask for something you need.

- Watch to see that all the condiments have been passed.

- Unfold a luncheon napkin entirely across your lap. A dinner napkin is unfolded only in half.

- Place your napkin in your chair if you have to leave the table during the meal.

- Eat at a moderate speed.

- Make sure that you do not make the others wait forever for you to finish your meal.

- Do not replace any used silverware on the table.

- Watch the host or hostess for beginnings and endings.

- Cut one bite at a time.

- Eat quietly, not making noise with your mouth or silverware.

Tips on Tipping

- *Bartender.* If you are drinking in the bar, leave $1.00 or 15 percent (or round up the bill to the next dollar when paying for a round at a time).

- *Bellman or airport skycap.* $1.00 per bag. If you require special service, $5.00 on arrival ensures good service.

- *Cafeteria.* Tip only if the person assists you with your tray to your seat ($1.00).

- *Captain/headwaiter.* Tip 5 percent of the bill. (You will find a separate box for the captain on the restaurant charge slip. Also, 15 percent still goes to your personal waiter.)

- *Carwash.* Look for a tipping box (50 cents to $1.00).

- *Caterer.* This is included in the service charge; if not, 15 percent of the catering charge, given in a lump sum to the manager, to be divided among the staff.

- *Chambermaid.* $1.00 per night per person. Leave it in an envelope marked, "Maid."

- *Cloakroom attendant.* If there is no charge, tip $1.00. If there is a charge, round up to the nearest dollar.
- *Complimentary pickup service.* Tipping is not customary unless the worker helps with your luggage (then tip $2.00).
- *Concierge.* Tip $5.00 to $20.00 on arrival if you want to be "fawned over." Tip $2.00 to $10.00 per service or $5.00 to $50.00 on departure. (This depends on the hotel, the length of stay, and the amount of service provided. Services include changing air reservations, obtaining hot theater seats, securing dinner reservations at the last minute, etc.)
- *Deliveries.* Tip 50 cents to $1.00.
- *Doorman.* Always tip for getting a taxi ($1.00). Do not tip if he simply opens the door for you.
- *Fishing/hunting guides.* Tip $5.00 for a one-day trip, $10.00 for a weekend, and $20.00 for up to a week.
- *Golf caddies.* Tip 15 to 20 percent of green fees for 18 holes.
- *Hair stylists.* Do not tip the owner. Tip 10 to 15 percent of bill otherwise. The person who washes your hair receives $1.00. (If you frequent a shop and the owner is your stylist, remember him or her with a gift at Christmas.)
- *Hospital staff.* Never appropriate, but a gift on departure to say "Thank you" to a particular nurse or aide is appropriate.
- *Instructor (ski, tennis, golf, etc.).* Not ordinarily tipped. If you are especially pleased, perhaps a drink, a dinner, or a bottle of wine.
- *Maitre d'.* Two reasons to tip: (1) to get a good table and (2) to become a favored regular. Tip $10 to $20 in a handshake.

- *Parking attendant/valet.* Tip $1.00 to $2.00 normally; in Los Angeles, tip $2.00 to $3.00.

- *Room service waiter.* Tip $1.00 to $5.00 if a service charge has been included; 15 percent of the bill otherwise. Shoe shine: 50 cents to $1.00.

- *Sommelier/wine steward.* Tip $3.00 to $5.00 per bottle or 15 percent of wine bill, given directly to the wine steward. Deduct wine cost from dinner bill if wine bill is not presented separately.

- *Taxi.* Tip 15 percent of fare.

- *Waiter/waitress.* Tip 15 to 20 percent of bill. If you have been unhappy with the service, reduce the tip to 10 percent, and let the server know why.

- *Washroom attendant.* Usually a coin dish is present to leave 50 cents (unless extra attention at a luxury hotel—$1.00).

TIPS ON ATTENDING OFFICIAL COMPANY FUNCTIONS

One of the biggest mistakes a career professional can make is to ignore an invitation to a company function. If management goes out of its way to invite you to a picnic, holiday party, or maybe a shareholder meeting, consider it an honor and show up (yes, that Woody Allen 90 percent of life, again). Right or wrong, company executives consider it a sign of disrespect if you blow off a social event. Just so you know.

Here are some other tips to make the most of your corporate socializing:

Stay cool. Many a career has been short-circuited by a high-wire performance at a corporate holiday party. Who hasn't heard of a coworker uncorking a few too many spirited beverages and making like Bluto in *Animal House*? What "Lampshade Larry" doesn't know—or is too pickled to notice—is that top management uses company outings as a litmus test for potential managers. And while they may not remember a name, boardroom types always remember a face.

Dress your best. Dressing like Britney Spears or Mick Jagger will get you noticed all right—but for all the wrong reasons. Remember, we're going for professionalism here. Save the leather and lace for Saturday night.

Converse outside the corporate box. Business is business, but don't overdo it at the big shindig. Managers don't always want to talk about the firm—they may want to discuss the latest Harrison Ford flick, the most recent issue of *Time,* or simply what Letterman's top 10 included last night. We all know people who can't talk about anything but business, and we know how slowly the clock ticks when we can't get away from them. Don't subject anyone to your take on the company's annual report. If you insist, chances are that you'll find yourself standing by yourself a lot. Above all, be positive when conversing with others. Mark Twain once said that he could live for two months on one good compliment. That's good enough for me.

Please allow me to introduce myself. Oliver Wendell Holmes once famously boiled down business functions for all time as simply, "giggle-gabble-gobble-git." Not to correct such a giant figure, but there's a bit more to them than this. Company parties are great opportunities to introduce yourself to your firm's bigwigs. Many employees, nervous or shy, don't take advantage. But if you keep ignoring face-time opportunities with the brass, you're decreasing your chances of gaining visibility with the people who count. When you see an opportunity to greet a bigwig, walk up, introduce yourself, extend a firm handshake, thank him or her for the invitation, and excuse yourself. If he or she asks you to stay for a minute, that's great. In general, however, don't take up too much time—just enough to break the ice.

No pay, no play. Certain subjects are taboo at company functions. Salary—specifically your dissatisfaction with your paycheck—is one of them. Bringing it up with management at a party demonstrates an appalling lapse in judgment on your part.

A Quickie Etiquette Quiz

1. In the business arena,
   a. Only men should stand for handshaking and all introductions.
   b. Only women should stand for handshaking and all introductions.
   c. It is not necessary for men or women to stand for handshaking or introductions.
   d. Both men and women should stand for handshaking and introductions.
2. To show confidence and authority during a handshake, use
   a. The bone crusher.
   b. The limp fish.
   c. The glove.
   d. The fingertip holder.
   e. The web to web.

Continued

3. For easy reading, one's name badge should be worn
   a. On the left shoulder.
   b. On the right shoulder.
   c. On the left hip.
   d. Around one's neck.
4. You are dining in a restaurant and you accidentally drop your fork on the floor, so you
   a. Pick it up, wipe it off, and use it anyway.
   b. Pick it up, give it to the server, and ask him or her to bring you another one.
   c. Leave it on the floor and ask the server to bring you another one.
   d. Leave it on the floor and use your neighbor's fork while he or she is not looking.
5. While seated next to someone at dinner, you notice the man on your left eating your bread from your bread plate, so you
   a. Tell him he made a mistake and then you ask for your bread back.
   b. Don't say anything and you eat from your other neighbor's bread plate.
   c. Don't say anything and try to convince yourself that you didn't need that piece of bread anyway.
   d. Ask the server for another roll and use the side of your dinner plate.
6. A woman's handbag, if it's small, can be placed on
   a. A desk.
   b. A boardroom table.
   c. A restaurant table.
   d. All of the above.
   e. None of the above.
7. If you have something lodged in your teeth and you want to remove it, you should
   a. Take your knife when no one is looking and remove it promptly with the blade.
   b. Raise your napkin to your mouth and discreetly use a Sweet 'n Low packet or your business card to remove it.
   c. Politely ask your server for a toothpick.

Continued

d. Excuse yourself and go to the restroom to pick your teeth in private.

8. You bite into a piece of meat that is tough and very difficult to chew, so you
    a. Pretend to wipe your mouth and deposit the meat into your napkin.
    b. Use two fingers or your fork to remove the meat and place it on the edge of your plate or underneath a piece of parsley.
    c. Swallow it and hope you don't choke.
    d. None of the above.

9. The best way to meet people and "work a room" is to
    a. Head for the bar or the buffet immediately on arrival.
    b. Introduce yourself to two people who are deep in conversation.
    c. Look confident, stand in the center of the room, and wait for someone interesting to approach you.
    d. Introduce yourself to groups of three or more.
    e. Stick close to only those you know very well.

10. When you are finished eating, your napkin should be
    a. Folded loosely and placed on the right side of your plate.
    b. Folded loosely and placed on the left side of your plate.
    c. Folded loosely and placed in the center of your plate.
    d. Folded like a dove or a pirate's hat and placed on the seat of your chair.

Answers

    1. d
    2. e
    3. b
    4. c
    5. c or d
    6. e
    7. d
    8. b
    9. d
   10. b

TIPS ON E-MAIL COMMUNICATIONS

With e-mail, the medium is truly the message. E-mail is a godsend for harried workers and a great way to develop business contacts both inside and outside the firm.

Often, though, e-mail is too fast and too anonymous for its own good. By its faceless nature and its tendency toward instant gratification, e-mail is a tempting tool to create havoc and bad will in the office.

The thing about e-mail is that even though it's electronically based, it's still the written word and has staying power. It's a written record that you may wish you'd never sent.

If you're a bit confused by e-mail, join the club. It's a new medium that's still working on its manners, and we're all getting the hang of it. But here are some ways to speed up the learning process a bit:

> *Lose the "emoticons."* You know those annoying little keyword happy faces, grins, and salutations? Yeah, me too. People try to use them to convey a sense of openness and warmth and frequently get the opposite effect. Treat an e-mail like you would a letter you'd write. Be yourself, but since this is business correspondence we're talking about, be professional. And no happy faces!

> *Be natural.* It's perfectly okay to preface a business e-mail with a homey touch. If you are sending an e-mail to Stan in marketing and you know that his wife just gave birth to a bouncing baby boy, congratulate him and his new family. People appreciate the human touch, especially in a soulless environment like cyberspace.

> *Don't whale on e-mail.* Don't be one of those office types who's always passing along stale jokes and sugar-sweet homilies. Send e-mail only when you have to and be respectful of other people's time.

Rapid response beats the old digital delay. You wouldn't be thrilled if a coworker ignored your phone calls, so don't be surprised if someone holds your feet to the fire because you've been slow in replying to e-mails. Rule of thumb? One day to return an e-mail, even if it's just to say, "I'm swamped right now, but I will help you out when I get a breather." Use autoreply if you go on vacation or are sick for a few days. This lets people know why you may be delayed in responding.

Be sensitive. There are some times when e-mail is inappropriate. You'd never deliver bad news such as a layoff or the loss of a major client via e-mail unless you were a coward. Real managers deliver the heavy stuff face to face. If you can't get face to face, a phone call is okay.

Meat'n'potatoes. Here are a few mechanical things a good e-mail should include every time:

- A subject label in the header
- A thorough proofread
- Your phone and fax number

Also, remember to never

- Send (or forward) racist, sexual, or pornographic materials.
- Gossip or criticize others in an e-mail, because it may come back to haunt you in the form of defamation or libel charges.
- Write in all capital letters. This is the online equivalent of shouting.
- Send angry or abusive e-mails. They may embarrass you later or, worse, lead to a harassment charge. Remember: Think twice, click once.

- Have an unprofessional e-mail address. Anything cute is not professional. SoftwareBabe@yahoo.com may be a crowd pleaser in some circles but not in the executive boardroom.

OFFICE PHONE ETIQUETTE

Thanks to e-mail, we're spending less time on the telephone, so we still need to spruce up on our phone skills. Here are a few quick tips to keep in mind at the workplace:

Whenever possible, answer the phone yourself. People want to know that you're accessible.

Be prompt in your call-backs. Good business etiquette dictates that all telephone calls be returned within 24 hours.

No rush job. It's a funny thing about leaving voice mail messages. We all think that a bomb is going to detonate unless we leave the message within five seconds. Relax. If you rush through your message, people may not get your name and number. A tip: Write down your name and number as you say it—which is what the other person will be doing. This should slow you down enough so that there's no mistaking your message.

Be informative. If you receive a voice mail from a coworker looking for information, feel free to leave that information on her voice mail. This is what technology is for—to save us all time.

No hangups. A top phone etiquette pet peeve is making a call, getting a voice mail response, and then hanging up without leaving a message. This is akin to rolling up to McDonald's drive-through window and taking off when the clerk asks for your order. In addition, in the age of "star 69" and screened phone calls, people will know it's you anyway and wonder about your motives if you hang up before leaving a message.

Can the speakerphone. Whoever said that technology was both a curse and a blessing might have had a cubicle next to a "speakerphoniac." They're loud, they're obtrusive, and they're everywhere. Only use a speakerphone when you're sure you're alone or you are in a place where you can close the door. And let the other party know that they're on a speakerphone. They may have points to make to you and you alone and don't want other ears listening in.

Cell out. If you're in a meeting, taking a cell phone call is akin to belching or humming the theme song to *Gilligan's Island.* In other words, it is a big faux pas. Place your phone on mute or vibrate or turn it off completely. Coworkers, clients, and the like demand and deserve your complete attention. Nobody likes playing second fiddle to a cell phone.

Don't assume. If you were visiting a new client at his office, you'd probably stop by the reception area and introduce yourself first. Likewise, when you make a phone call and get a receptionist or secretary, identify yourself and tell her the basic nature of your call. In this way, you'll be sure you're getting the right person or department, and the person you're trying to reach will be able to pull up the appropriate information and help you more efficiently. Contrarily, when you're on the receiving end of a phone call, identify yourself and your department. Answer the phone with some enthusiasm or at least warmth even if you are being interrupted; the person on the other end doesn't know this.

Twelve Tips for Better Business Manners

1. Unlike social etiquette, business etiquette is genderless or gender-neutral. Therefore, both men and women always should stand when introduced and offer a firm handshake.

2. The first person to the door opens it.

3. Always make introductions; if you forget someone's name, apologize and ask for the name again.

4. Introduce people in business based on rank, not gender (introduce the person of lower rank to the person of higher rank). The client or customer is always the most important person. Begin the introduction by identifying the most important person—the client—first.

5. Always refer to someone as Mister or Ms until he or she asks you to use a first name.

6. First impressions are formed in four to seven seconds. Make sure your handshake is firm!

7. Hugs and kisses are inappropriate in the business environment (unless you're in Hollywood). The handshake is the only acceptable physical contact between men and women in a business setting.

8. When entering an office or conference room for a meeting, do not sit down until you have asked the person who called the meeting where he or she wants you to sit.

9. Do not put your briefcase, handbag, papers, or keys on the table during a meal or meeting; place them on the floor beside you or under your seat.

10. Never let your cell phone ring during a meal or meeting; set the phone on the vibrate mode.

11. A handwritten thank-you note to your customer will distinguish you from your competition.

12. Return voice mail, e-mail, and phone calls within 24 hours. If you don't have an appropriate reply, call and set up another time to communicate.

REALITY CHECK: POLISHED MANNERS MAKE FOR PROMOTED EXECUTIVES

Chuck Dorsey's friends kid him about his dining etiquette. The 40-something executive at a Wall Street trading firm is adamant about good table manners and expects his coworkers to follow suit. Napkin on the lap, elbows off the table, and silverware all in its proper place.

It wasn't always so. Dorsey grew up career-wise in a hustling Wall Street culture with little time for table manners and no concern about dribbling barbecue sauce down its collective chin.

"I remember not thinking a thing of ordering a big, juicy cheeseburger at a client lunch or taking bread from another person's basket," the now polished and successful business executive recalls. "Heck, I used to tuck my napkin under my chin like I was a 10-year-old at a family reunion."

Fortunately, Dorsey's wife, Jan, helped him become the paragon of virtue he is now at business and social functions by signing him up for etiquette classes at a local higher education center. "I learned that people often judge you by the way you present yourself in public," says Dorsey. "Holding your fork as if it were a pitchfork or clearing bread crumbs off your table with your hand makes you look like you just came out of a cave. I knew I was better than that, and it turns out I was."

Now when Dorsey sees a subordinate licking his soupspoon or overdoing it on the wine at a business function, he's quick to pull the young professional aside and deftly point out the error of his ways. "Invariably, they all thank me for it later," he says.

11

Choose Me: Grabbing the Brass Ring

It's no secret. To position yourself to be promoted and to charge ahead in your career, you have to make yourself indispensable in the workplace. Not only that, but you have to show initiative and take advantage of the opportunities that your work environment provides.

You have to move fast because these windows of opportunity open and close fast. But if you recognize an opportunity when you see it and you demonstrate a little resiliency and initiative, there's absolutely no reason why you can't grab the brass ring and have the career that you've hit the pillow many nights dreaming about. A little luck doesn't hurt either.

To illustrate what I mean, consider how some employees' resiliency and stick-to-itiveness (literally) have helped successful companies in the past to become household names.

- In 1879, Procter & Gamble's best-seller was candles. But the company was in trouble. Thomas Edison had invented the light bulb, and it looked as if candles would become obsolete. The company's fears became reality when the market for candles plummeted because now they were sold only for special occasions. While the outlook appeared to be bleak for Procter & Gamble, destiny played a dramatic part in pulling the struggling company from the clutches of bankruptcy. An employee at a small factory in Cincinnati forgot to turn off his candle-making machine when he went to lunch. The result? A frothing mass of lather filled with air bubbles. He almost threw the stuff away but instead decided to make it into soap. The soap floated. Thus Ivory soap was born and became the mainstay of the Procter & Gamble Company.

- How about the 3M Company, a company that historically has encouraged creativity on the part of its employees? The company allows its researchers to spend 15 percent of their time on any project that interests them. Some years ago, a scientist in 3M's commercial office took advantage of this 15 percent creative time. The scientist, Art Fry, came up with an idea for one of 3M's best-selling products. It seems that Mr. Fry dealt with a small irritation every Sunday as he sang in the church choir. After marking his pages in the hymnal with small bits of paper, the small pieces invariably would fall out all over the floor. Suddenly, an idea struck Fry. He remembered an adhesive developed by a colleague that everyone thought was a failure because it did not stick very well. He coated the adhesive on a paper sample and found not only that it was a good bookmark but also that it was great for writing notes. He also found that the notes stayed in place as long as one wanted them to and could be removed without damage to the underlying page. The product's name? The Post-it Note. It has since become one of the most widely used office products in the world.

As an aside, the Post-it Note almost didn't make it out of 3M, demonstrating that there's always room for intelligence in the executive suite. Distributors didn't seem to want the Post-its, and managers at 3M pointed to marketing surveys that indicated that customers wouldn't want them either. It wasn't until one bright marketing staffer sent the little note pads to company secretaries and administrative staffers at Fortune 500 companies that the Post-it Note finally created a buzz.

HOW TO GET PROMOTED

Just like the Procter & Gamble employee and 3M's Art Fry, you can make a difference at your company too. In doing so, you are also making a big difference in your career. In the examples just mentioned, both employees proved indispensable to their companies, which is the whole idea if you want to get promoted to that marketing post you've always desired or if you would like to have managerial responsibility for your own department, budget, and staff.

Granted, some promotions depend on timing. What works for a company today may not work for a company tomorrow. Take Winston Churchill. He was a political outcast in 1935. Yet, by 1940, he was leading England in World War II. Wrong place, wrong time in 1935. Right time, right place in 1940.

By and large, though, most promotions are given out to the people who want them the most, no matter what the timing. In this spirit, here's another dos and don'ts list on getting promoted. Follow it and you will have an edge when opportunities arise.

Dos

Do Be Prepared

As Johnny Carson once said, "Talent alone won't make you a success. Neither will being in the right place at the right time, unless you are ready. The most important question is: 'Are you ready?' So you have to ask yourself if you were presented with the opportunity of your lifetime tomorrow, what will it be . . . and will you be prepared to capitalize on it?"

Do Begin Early

I realize that the "begin early" thing has become something of a mantra in this book. But I say it with good reason. Starting as soon as possible to improve a workplace skill usually means that you'll reap the benefits of that work earlier too. Let's say you begin your career in the mailroom. The day your journey to the corner office begins when you are selected from among the other mail-room staffers as head of operations. Translation? It's never too early to be promoted.

Do Train Someone to Do Your Job

The best way to get promoted is to ensure that someone else knows how to do your job. Staffers are forever getting stuck, even though they deserve to move up, because their companies can't afford to uproot them from their current posts—nobody else can handle their responsibilities. The fact is that most promotions occur because people get pushed up from underneath, not pulled up from above. Your best bet is to train someone else to do your job so that you're free to move up in the world.

Do Be Able to Think on Your Feet

Management loves a quick thinker—and employees will allow themselves to be led by one.

Consider an old story about Daniel Webster. When Webster was a boy in the district school, he was not noted for his tidiness. Finally, his teacher, in despair, told him that if he appeared again with such dirty hands, she would trash him. He did appear the next day in the same condition. "Daniel," she said, "hold out your hand." Young Webster spat on his palm, rubbed it on the seat of his trousers, and held it out. The teacher surveyed it in disgust.

"Daniel," she said, "if you can find me another hand in this school that is dirtier than that, I will let you off."

Young Daniel promptly held out the other hand.

In doing so, he showed a glimpse of what America would later see from one of its most historical figures.

Do Make Your Weaknesses Your Strengths

Sometimes your biggest weakness can become your biggest strength. There's an old story about a 10-year-old boy who decided to study judo despite the fact that he had lost his left arm in a devastating car accident.

The boy began lessons with an old Japanese judo master. The boy was doing well, so he couldn't understand why, after three months of training, the master had taught him only one move.

"Sensei," the boy finally said, "Shouldn't I be learning more moves?"

"This is the only move you know, but this is the only move you'll ever need to know," the sensei replied.

Not quite understanding but believing in his teacher, the boy kept training. Several months later, the sensei took the boy to his first tournament. Surprising himself, the boy easily won his first two matches. The third match proved to be more difficult, but after some time, his opponent became impatient and charged; the boy deftly used his one move to win the match. Still amazed by his success, the boy was now in the finals.

This time, his opponent was bigger, stronger, and more experienced. For a while, the boy appeared to be overmatched. Concerned that the boy might get hurt, the referee called a time-out. He was about to stop the match when the sensei intervened.

"No," the sensei insisted, "Let him continue."

Soon after the match resumed, the boy's opponent made a critical mistake: He dropped his guard. Instantly, the boy used his move to pin him. The boy had won the match and the tournament. He was the champion.

On the way home, the boy and sensei reviewed every move in each and every match. Then the boy summoned the courage to ask what was really on his mind.

"Sensei, how did I win the tournament with only one move?"

"You won for two reasons," the sensei answered. "First, you've almost mastered one of the most difficult throws in all of judo. And second, the only known defense for that move is for your opponent to grip your left arm."

The boy's biggest weakness had become his biggest strength. He learned to shield his weaknesses by working on his strength, a lesson that's well worth applying in your career.

Do Bore in on the Bottom Line

Remember, those who get results get ahead. To move forward, create a new product or service or fix a problem.

Do Branch Out

President John F. Kennedy once said that "life isn't fair." He easily could have been talking about the contextual reasons people get promoted—reasons that often have little to do with accomplishments. Sometimes people get promoted who are less capable than you are. Most likely the reasons have nothing to do with your job performance. Your coworker may have been in the right place at the right time. She may have been phased out of one position and into a higher one as a result of a new company strategy. Or she may have shown a more diverse skill set than you. One way to nip this in the bud is to make sure that you branch out and learn as many different facets of your company as you can. Try volunteering to be on a cross-functional task force. Take advantage of company-paid education programs and attend some classes. Make your managers aware that you're doing these things. This could well give you the edge when a higher-paying, more prestigious post opens up.

Do Convince Your Firm to Create a New Job for You

You're multitalented. You're leadership material. You're chomping at the bit to move on up to that "dee-luxe apartment in the sky." If nothing's happening, why not study your company's needs and strategies and build a case for management to build a job that capitalizes on your unique capabilities?

A personal note: This actually happened to me. I was working for a business newsletter publishing company writing copy for mutual fund firms, brokerages, and banks. Most of my company's work was on the retail side—developing collateral geared toward individual investors and bank customers. We had an institutional side (newsletters geared to an institutional business audience, such as stock traders, financial advisors, and bank managers). But the institutional business was virtually an afterthought. Having spent five years on Wall Street trading desks right out of college, I volunteered to become an institutional editor and build up that side of the business. I had great contacts, I knew the lingo, and I knew what interested Wall Street's vast institutional audience. Management agreed and created the new position with me in mind. Very cool.

Do Get a Mentor

I did a whole chapter on this topic, but mentorships are worth mentioning again.

Why? Because with many promotions, the fix is in. Most managers know exactly whom they want to promote—and only that person gets real consideration.

Frequently, the person who gets promoted has worked with the hiring manager. It's unlikely that bosses will feel compelled to look elsewhere if they already know someone who can do the job. Sure, management may arrange a "beauty pageant" with plenty of "position available" memos flying around and cattle-call interviews with hoards of eager contestants streaming into the hiring manager's office. The fact is, though, that the search is usually over before it began. It's just window dressing.

Having a mentor can help you get into the inner circle instead of always being on the outside looking in. According to a University of Illinois study on business promotions, 81 percent of the participants promoted said that they had a mentoring relationship with someone higher in the company who used some clout on their behalf.

Do Learn How Past Executives Got to the Top

Here's a great idea: Make a list of all the executives who have held the job you want. Do a little digging (old annual reports and company newsletters are great, as are old-timers at your company), and find out how they got there. Also talk to people who have held the post you want. Find out what they did to succeed and what they would do differently. Discuss the mistakes they made, how they see the job evolving, and what steps you should take to promote yourself. Retrace their steps, and create footprints to follow. If your company's past marketing directors all made pit stops in sales and in public relations, maybe you should too.

Do Become Better at Your Boss's Job Than She Is

My corporate vacuum theory holds that if there is an empty spot, somebody's got to fill it. Thus, if your boss is promoted and the company is looking for someone to take her place and you know the job better than she does and can demonstrate it to management, then chances are office maintenance personnel will be changing the nameplate on your boss's door from hers to yours.

Do Become the Obvious Choice

When a position opens up, give hiring managers no option but to choose you. How? By doing things like training your replacement and learning your boss's job—things we've just talked about. It is also a good idea to read the same publications your boss reads, keep building a base of networking contacts, and know what the jobs at the next level entail.

In short, becoming the obvious choice isn't just about being capable at the job you're already doing. It also means having the knowledge and skills to do the job at the next level.

Do Learn Leadership Skills

People ask about the difference between a leader and a boss. According to former President Teddy Roosevelt, a leader works in the open, and a boss is covert. The leader leads, and the boss drives. Are you a leader or a driver?

Do Make an Appointment

There's nothing wrong with letting your workplace managers know that you want to be promoted. In fact, it's a good idea to talk to them—and only them—about it.

But do so discreetly. Meet with your supervisor and inform him that your desire is to move to the next level, and ask for an explanation of what the company is looking for in that position. Make an appointment with your supervisor beforehand. The last thing that you want to do is catch him off guard. Give your supervisor a chance to gather some thoughts in order to be able to map out exactly what your areas of opportunity are. This will help you both in the long run. Survival tip: Don't try this during your first week on the job. Prove yourself first.

Do See Things from Management's Point of View

Forward-thinking career professionals always see the big picture and always place themselves in management's position after a big, if controversial, decision has been made. Sometimes companies will elect to take a step back before they move forward, as computer networking giant EMC did in the 1990s, switching from a storage tape developer to a networking software company. You would have had difficulty convincing employees at the time that it was a good idea, but EMC rode the networking boom of the 1990s to its highest earnings ever. And many EMC employees got rich on stock options.

Do Have the Ability to Laugh—and Make Others Laugh

Nobody likes working for a pompous sourpuss. And since your job as a manager will be to motivate and persuade others to excel, this is a much easier task if you eschew the tough taskmaster route and keep things light and on an even keel. People will notice if you take yourself too seriously.

Don'ts

Avoid these traps and pitfalls to increase your chances of landing that big promotion.

Don't Gossip

Careful, the office grapevine can strangle you. Management has no use for managers with loose lips. If you're labeled a loudmouth, better start looking for a new company.

Don't Overlook Compassion

When you show you care about others, they'll show that they care about you. So don't be reluctant to forge personal relationships within the organization. Send birthday cards, and call someone who is ill to wish him well. People will remember how well you treated them and usually will reward you for it. You'll appreciate these contacts as you move up in the world.

Don't Complain

Believe me, you don't have a monopoly on griping about your job. Everybody has something to complain about, and many do. Don't be one of them. It's an energy-sapping exercise anyway with no point to it. In addition, the walls have ears, and your moaning and groaning will reach the wrong people. If the company's managers hear about your unhappiness, they may well reason that you're looking for a new job. Therefore, why should they promote you when you're not going to be around in six months?

Don't Be a Pessimist

A pessimist is someone who can look at the land of milk and honey and see only calories and cholesterol. Always try to see the bright side of things. In his day, Walt Disney liked to tell the story about 10 of his managers who didn't think an idea about a new cartoon mouse would fly. Today Mickey Mouse is one of the most instantly recognizable images on earth.

Don't Hog the Spotlight

People who steal credit for work they didn't do make enemies with long memories. It all comes down to business ethics. Once you're stuck on the flypaper, you're stuck. You won't rise any higher than your present job if you develop a reputation for hogging all the credit. In fact, a strong case can be made that management prefers someone who takes blame for a mistake. It shows that the person wants to be held accountable for his work and is learning and gaining experience in the process. If you want to move up to the next level, get a reputation for taking genuine pleasure in the success of others. Encourage, teach, promote, and support.

Don't Smoke

I don't and won't pass judgment on smokers. I will say, though, that smokers are low on the list of employees managers like to promote (unless you work at a cigarette company, and even then, who knows?). People who smoke at work are likely to be marked down on job performance because of it, reducing both the probability of their promotion and their income. It may not be fair, but when the big boss sees you huddled outside the office in mid-February, puffing away in freezing weather, he may wonder about both your state of mind and your dependability.

DIDN'T GET THE JOB? TIME TO REGROUP AND RENEW YOUR COMMITMENT

Sometimes things don't work out as we planned. This doesn't mean we give up.

Look at Winston Churchill, whom I've already mentioned in this chapter as an example of someone who made the most of his window of opportunity. An opportunist, true, but Churchill had no quit in him either. Here was a man who suffered political setback after political setback in his country only to finally become Prime Minister of Great Britain. Even then he had to take on the mighty German army and rally his countrymen time after time when things looked bleak. His leadership skills stood the test of time.

In his later years, Churchill was asked to speak to the graduating class at Oxford University. Following his introduction, he rose, walked to the podium, and said simply, "Never, never, never give up." Then he sat down.

Churchill didn't quit, and neither should you.

Therefore, if you don't get that promotion, find out why, and plan a new avenue of attack. Again, it might not be your fault at all. You might learn that the company decided not to hire anyone for the position or that a tight economy forced your company to freeze promotions for a while. Retrace your steps to see if there isn't something that you can do differently when a promotional opportunity comes around again. Ask your supervisor what you can do to get the job next time.

If you believe that you didn't get a fair shake and never will from your current company, by all means begin looking around at other companies. If you've applied the skills and strategies that I've just outlined, believe me, there is someone out there who considers you management material and will give you a chance to prove it. Probably lots of people.

MORE QUALITIES MANAGEMENT CONSIDERS WHEN HANDING OUT PROMOTIONS

I've spent the bulk of this book outlining the traits that enable professionals to get the kinds of careers they want. Let's focus on some of the more hands-on skills that executives can't do without.

Be a Solid Communicator

A good manager not only possesses the skills of persuasion and motivation, but he or she also must master the subtle nuances of body language and learn to read between the lines when interacting with both staffers and upper management.

One good way to practice these skills is to observe successful managers in the workplace and see how they handle people. Chances are that they're good listeners, accomplished public speakers, and comfortable in one-on-one meetings. While you're at it, take a public speaking course at your local college or higher education center. Or join Toastmasters, a public speaking group that trains professionals in the art of public speaking. This organization has offices all over the United States.

Can You Lead?

Like the college football running back who gets to the National Football League and can't believe how much faster everything moves at that level, it's a different world in management than it is as a rank-and-file employee.

Just think how hard it was to change yourself, and you'll understand how hard it can be to change others. To be this type of leader, you have to determine where you want your troops to go and then get up and go there with them. Look at former Chrysler Chairman Lee Iacocca. The man had his critics, but he led a $13 billion company back from the brink of bankruptcy and saved 80,000 jobs in the process. He did it through strength of personality and a remarkable ability to persuade people to follow his leadership.

Embrace Diversity

No two people are alike, even in the same workplace. Good managers recognize this and don't try to employ a "one size fits all" managerial style. The best executives adapt to all kinds of personalities, using a "tough love" approach on someone with a thick hide and a warm, parenting demeanor with the more sensitive workplace types.

Savvy leaders take the time to learn what motivates some employees and what motivates others. This "leader of the pack" instinct separates leaders from followers. Knowing how to manage people on an individual basis may be the most important trait a leader can have.

Are You Committed?

The people who make the best leaders are totally focused on meeting their goals. They won't let anything stand in their way. Sometimes we think we are committed, but we aren't. Ever hear the tale of the chicken and the pig? The two were talking one day about commitment. The chicken said, "I'm committed to giving eggs every morning." The pig responded, "Giving eggs isn't a commitment; it's participation. But giving ham—now that's a commitment."

THE MOST IMPORTANT THING FOR A MANAGER TO REMEMBER

There's an old saying that spells out how simply successful managers should think (although anyone can benefit). It's called "The Most Important Words."

The six most important words: *"I admit that I was wrong."*

The five most important words: *"You did a great job."*

The four most important words: *"What do you think?"*

The three most important words: *"Could you please . . ."*

The two most important words: *"Thank you."*

The most important word: *"We."*

The least important word: *"I."*

12

Fifty Career Survival Tips You Can Take to the Corner Office

In the course of writing this book—or any book for that matter—there's only so much room and so much time to get everything you want inside of it. In the first 11 chapters of this book you've read about the absolute key issues to address and critical moves to make to give yourself the best opportunity to grab that dream job you've always wanted and forge a career that will make you happy. I mean, isn't that what it's all about?

But there's so much good stuff I wanted to add that I couldn't find room for it all. This is why I saved this chapter for last. To augment the career success cornerstones I've discussed already—things like being a gold-collar worker, leveraging office politics to your advantage, and great ways to get promoted—I'm adding 50 great career tips here that can add luster and polish to the lean, mean career advancement machine that is you.

These tips are a bit random, but they are all extremely useful. Take a look and see what I mean.

1. OPERATE UNDER THE RADAR

Some coworkers might resent the fact that you've developed a good relationship with your boss. In general, to hell with them. But if a stray comment or two bothers you, there's a good way to get in good with your boss without raising too many eyebrows. One way is to volunteer. At night or early in the morning—when only you and your supervisor are in the office—ask if there's anything you can do to help her. Also ask, "How can I make a larger contribution?" It's contributions that make successful careers, at least in the long run. Never be just a warm body. It's the proactive people who are promoted and then promoted again.

2. BE AN EFFECTIVE TEAM MEMBER

Many companies today operate under the team concept, where groups of uniquely skilled coworkers forge formal alliances to contribute to the bottom line. But how do you best get along with team members and get noticed by management?

Easy. First, know your role on the team. If you work for an advertising agency and you're a graphic designer, don't tell the copywriter how to do her job. And vice versa. Remember the golden rule about sharing credit and avoiding gossip and back stabbing. Be professional—if the others aren't, it will all come out in the wash.

3. ASK FOR HELP

You've got a great new idea for a product, but it's still sitting in your bottom drawer. The thing is, you'll never get credit unless you spread the word. The political dynamics of your company may make this easy or hard. But you can network over the Internet to quickly share your ideas, creations, or inventions. And if you choose the correct forum, you can get feedback not only from a small circle of friends or decision makers but also from all around the world.

4. JOIN A PROFESSIONAL ORGANIZATION

Keep your knowledge current and your contacts fresh by joining a professional organization. Whether it's your local Chamber of Commerce or an industry trade group, there are few better ways to remain plugged in than by hooking up with people who can help you.

5. LEARN ANOTHER LANGUAGE

Parlez-vous français? Why not? In an increasingly global-oriented economy, the plum assignments often go to the people who can travel overseas and speak the native language. Why let an opportunity pass to go to France to run the new marketing effort there because you can't say "Get me Fishbein on the hop!" in French?

6. GET AN ADVANCED DEGREE

People who say that college degrees are overrated and that people skills and capability count the most in a career are either working on their fifth martini or haven't got a degree.

If a college degree didn't matter, then all the Harvard Business School graduates would be working for all the high school graduates. Not that I wouldn't pay to see that scenario unfold, but it will never happen. A college diploma—or better yet, an advanced degree—is the ticket to the executive suite. Even if it's a drool bucket wearing Neanderthal clutching that diploma, chances are there's another drool bucket wearing Neanderthal from the same college waiting to take care of him.

7. BE ETHICAL

Would you trust someone who you didn't think was ethical? Would you work for or buy a product from such a person? Employees under pressure to perform must be careful not to put members of their teams in situations where their ethics could be compromised. People who cut corners or take the easy way out are the last to be considered for promotions.

8. TAKE ON MORE RESPONSIBILITY

This one's a no-brainer. If you want to get more in the way of pay or prestige, give more. One way is to volunteer to head up a new project. If it succeeds, you'll look like leadership material if you give the lion's share of credit to members of the team. If the project fails, take the responsibility but absorb the lessons. Another option is to be the messenger who brings bad news rather than trying to conceal problems. Most of the time company managers will thank you for bringing a problem to their attention.

9. KEEP TRACK OF YOUR INDUSTRY

Management and coworkers alike appreciate a heads-up employee who knows what the competition is doing. Subscribe to *Fortune* or

Business Week, read all the industry newsletters, attend as many industry functions as you can. Sign up for industry chat rooms. Be agreeable and engaging to everyone you meet, but be listening. Your company will love you for it,

10. CONSIDER RELOCATING

Be open to the idea of changing locales. When I worked on Wall Street, I was young and single—a great time to volunteer (in my case) for posts in New York City, Boston, and San Francisco. Great cities all, and I learned a lot about my company and industry in going (I made a slew of new contacts too). Remember, as your company grows, the number of job positions and national presence increase. Find out if the company needs a manager to cover a new sales territory or oversee the opening of a new regional office. The job might just be temporary, but it may also be what moves you up the corporate ladder. When you go, think of it as an adventure. It might prove to be the time of your life.

11. GETTING BACK INTO THE GAME AFTER HAVING A BABY

Many new moms want to stay home for a while after having a baby or two. Some stay home for years after starting a family.

So what do you do if you are a mother who wants back in after having been away from the workplace for six or seven years? One solution is to work part time until you get your bearings and your family adjusts to your being away from the home. Another is to job share with another employee. Here, both of you have the same job but you split it time-wise. Ask your company if these solutions are available. And if you're the entrepreneurial sort who still doesn't want to leave the nest, start a home-based business. Many such businesses are inexpensive to establish, and you can still be there for the little ones when they come home from school.

12. ALLEVIATING KEYBOARD "CLUTCH" CONDITIONS

So you say that you work in front of a computer all day and that your back is threatening to sue you for nonsupport ("If the chair doesn't fit, you must acquit"). Try these tips to help reduce back and body stress:

- Relax your shoulders, lift your torso tall, and keep your head upright and your chin level.

- Keep your ears in line with your shoulders and your shoulders in line with your hips. There should be a natural S curve in your spine.

- Use your abdominal muscles to maintain good posture. This reduces the strain on your lower back.

- When sitting at a computer, keep your feet flat on the floor and use a chair that supports your lower back. Your keyboard should be positioned at waist high so that your forearms can remain level with your wrists held straight.

- Take frequent breaks—at least every 20 to 30 minutes if you perform repetitive tasks. Take a moment to stretch the muscles you are working, as well as those that help maintain proper posture: neck, shoulders, arms, fingers, and back.

13. ACT LIKE AN ENTREPRENEUR AT THE OFFICE

Even though you answer to a boss and work in a cubicle, try to be entrepreneurial in your work life. Proactively ask for a raise, pursue a promotion, or solicit a transfer. Take the new job or join the startup if given the chance. When a new idea is raised, don't point out how similar plans have failed before. Instead, voice your enthusiasm and offer ways to avoid past pitfalls. Remember, in the end it's "You, Inc."

14. BE READY TO CHANGE ON THE FLY

Be a quick-change artist to get ahead. Adaptability is what's needed to get ahead in a quickly changing business world. The highly specialized job that's hot today may be outmoded tomorrow, which is why continually learning new skills and providing new services are so important.

15. BE COMPUTER SAVVY

No matter where you hang your career hat, you have to have computer skills. The more the better. Fishermen have computers on boats, and farmers have them on their tractors. There's no excuse not to be computer savvy. Take a class at a local higher education center, or learn some new skills on the Internet.

16. HAVE AN UNDERSTANDING ABOUT OVERTIME

Many professionals think that they need to burn the midnight oil to get ahead. To me, this is a hangover from the dot-com craze that probably will burn you out faster than it will burnish your workplace image. As a rule, tell your employer before you're hired—or as soon as possible after you're hired—that you will put in a good, solid workday. If emergencies, deadline, or peak periods arise, you'll stay late. Be direct about it, and reach an agreement about your hours before it's too late and your company starts taking advantage of you.

17. REHEARSE AND FINISH FIRST

Going on a big job interview? One way to nail the job is to practice with a mock interview. Mock interviews are conducted as actual interviews, and they give you the practice you need to polish your interviewing skills. Another suggestion would be to role-play with friends using some of the sample questions in the next tip and have them give you feedback.

18. SAMPLE JOB INTERVIEW QUESTIONS YOU'LL LIKELY BE ASKED

When you go on a job interview, be prepared to answer these questions:

- Tell me about yourself.
- Why did you choose to attend (*fill in the name of your college*)?
- Why did you decide to major in (*fill in your major*)?
- Could you compare your team player versus entrepreneurial spirit for me?
- How did you hear about this company?
- What do you know about this company, and what interests you the most?
- Why did you leave your last job?
- What are your short- and long-term goals? How will you benefit by achieving them? What plans have you made to achieve them?
- Tell me about a few of your accomplishments.
- What are your greatest strengths/skills?

- Why are you interested in this particular job?
- What motivates you to put forth your greatest effort?
- What do you think you can do for us that someone else can't do just as well?
- What qualities should a successful manager possess?
- What else do you think I should know about you?
- What would you like to know about this company?

19. SOME JOB INTERVIEW QUESTIONS YOU WANT TO ASK

Score points on your job interview by asking these attention-getting questions:

- How did you start with the organization?
- Could you describe the work environment?
- To whom does the position report?
- How many subordinates, if any, report to the position?
- What has become of the person who previously held the position? Is it possible to talk to him or her?
- What are you looking for in a successful candidate?
- What are the objectives for the person hired in this position?
- What would be a typical first-year assignment?
- What promotional opportunities will be available to me, assuming that I do an exceptional job?
- Does the company have a promotion from within policy?
- What are the company's objectives for the next year?
- What is your timetable for filling this position?

- Have I told you everything you need to know about my background? Do you have any concerns?
- What is the next step?

20. KEEP A JOURNAL

Putting your thoughts, accomplishments, and goals down on paper is a great way to monitor your career progress and establish a record of your past achievements. Taking five minutes a day and writing a brief paragraph about how your day went is an important success strategy. Simply use a lined hardbound journal or start a new computer file and memorialize your success and learning experiences. Bonus point: A journal is a great legacy to pass on to your children.

21. THE 30-MINUTE MANAGER

Is your workday going according to plan? It will if you carve out 10 minutes first thing in the morning and make sure that you have a written daily game plan. Around lunchtime, set aside another 10-minute block to review how your morning went and make minor adjustments in your afternoon task list. Lastly, set aside 10 minutes at the end of your day to review how effective you were in accomplishing your tasks.

22. TRY TO BE LOYAL

A recent survey of chief executive officers (CEOs) found that 85 percent of the respondents ranked employee loyalty first among traits in valued employees. The reason? Most CEOs surveyed found that it was in the shortest supply among their staff. Thus, even if you're not thrilled with your firm or your job, don't go public with it. Strap on a smile and pride yourself on being a team player. This might just be the key to advancing to better things.

23. STARTING A NEW JOB? BE VISIBLE

Most people—myself included—start new jobs with their heads down and noses to the grindstone. Months may go by before you come out of your shell and get noticed by colleagues. Don't make this mistake. When you start a new job, go out of your way to introduce yourself to everyone, and focus on remembering everyone's name. Network up—meet the leaders, the key players, and the movers and shakers in your group, right up to the top. Participate in meetings, and be part of the team from the very first day.

24. KNOW YOUR COMPANY BETTER THAN ANYONE ELSE

One great way to get noticed by the muckety-mucks upstairs is to bone up on your company. This includes not only knowing what your company does, what it sells, and who its competitors are but also making note of what departments are where and what names are on the doors. Talk with someone from a different department every day to learn the various functions of the operation. Pretty soon you'll earn a reputation as a valuable and dependable information source.

25. HOLD YOUR FIRE

Every so often you'll have to disagree with somebody at work. When you must include criticism in a written message, draft the contents and wait a day before you transmit the message. You may want to sleep on what you said before sending it.

26. MIRROR, MIRROR

Everybody has a bad day. If you're growling and groaning, however, managers and coworkers will notice. Here's a tip: Keep a mirror by the phone. When it rings and you're in a snappish mood, hold the mirror to your face. Even if the other party can't see you, you'll know how they perceive your disposition by the face looking back at you in the mirror.

27. BE CIVIC-MINDED

Former Massachusetts Congressman Tip O'Neill once said that all politics is local. This is true in business too. Companies like to be good members of their communities and put on a happy civic face. Help your firm by reading your local newspapers and talking to community members to find out what's going on in your neck of the woods. If there's a negative buzz about your company from community members, trust me, the big wigs will want to know about it. Plugging into the community also can help bring quality people aboard when new jobs open up. People will value you for this reason alone when the job market opens up and the best people are in demand.

28. SURE-FIRE CONVERSATION STOPPERS

If you're talking to coworkers and are exhibiting these nonverbal no-no's, you might get a reputation as someone who's a poor communicator:

- Eye rolling
- Sighing

- Rapid-fire foot tapping and leg bouncing, or "sewing machine knee"
- Interrupting
- Glancing away from the person who is speaking even for a split second
- Head nodding

29. MEETING TIP: WORK THE ROOM BEFOREHAND

Smart professionals know how to get the most out of meetings. One way is to work the room beforehand and chat with some of the participants prior to the meeting to get a feel for their attitudes regarding the information you are presenting.

30. EYE SPY

When conversing with coworkers, look them square in the eye. Dialogue experts say that this demonstrates a take-charge personality that demands respect—in other words, the trait of a great executive.

31. PUT YOURSELF IN THE CUSTOMER'S PLACE

If you're in a sales position or handle customers on a regular basis, try to open up and see things from their point of view. A client who's complaining about a late shipment of products could very well be late in shipping your products to his clients. Ask yourself before any discussion with a client, "What if I were in his shoes?" Clients will rave about you to management if you can pull this off on a regular basis.

32. LEARN ABOUT CUSTOMERS AND EARN MORE BUSINESS

Remember personal details about your customers, such as birthdays, children's names, and accomplishments. All clients want products or services that work and solve their problems. But most clients, given the choice between two capable companies, will choose the one that forges the best relationship. A little of the human touch will do just this.

33. GOING AWAY ON VACATION? HERE'S HOW TO LEAVE YOUR WORKPLACE

Some workers are actually frazzled by the notion of going away on vacation. No, not because of the potential sunburn or bouts with the local island water supply. Because of what will happen at work while they're away.

But if you're prepared, there's no reason to get all jelly in the knees. Before you go, complete critical deadlines and notify all coworkers and vendors that you'll be away. Set up contingency plans with staff members, and appoint a single person to serve as your work filter. If your boss insists on you leaving a number to be reached, give him your e-mail address. In this way, you can check once a day on the resort's computer room (most have them now) or on your personal digital assistant (PDA) or laptop, and you won't have to worry about the phone ringing on the eighteenth green.

34. WORK ON YOUR PUBLIC SPEAKING SKILLS

Most executives are used to getting up on their feet and riffing. You too should grow accustomed to public speaking. Here are some ways to do just that:

- Volunteer to lead a discussion group for your department—before you're put on the spot and have to.
- Take speaking engagements with your professional association or local Chamber of Commerce.
- Give a speech at your local Kiwanis or Rotary luncheon.
- Be the speaker at the next meeting of your book discussion group or investment club.
- Join Toastmasters.

35. UPDATE YOUR ROLODEX

If there are contacts in your files with whom you haven't spoken in a long time, give them a call to touch base.

36. DRESS-CODE ALERT

Every time you dress for work, you send a message by what colors you're wearing (no, I'm not running out of material and making this up). Here's the sweet and lowdown on dress-code color schemes:

- Brown: A natural color. Whether camel, khaki, tan, or taupe, brown projects reliability, durability, comfort, and warmth.
- Gray: Associated with intelligence, confidence in the future, and security. Other shades include charcoal and silver.
- Black: Reflects sophistication, confidence, wealth, and power. Paired with white, black conveys truth and confidence.
- Navy blue: Dependability, reliability, and strength. Navy is a flattering color that all ages, shapes, and sizes can wear well. A navy suit combined with a white shirt conveys an air of trust and honesty.

- Red: The color of aggression, sexuality, dominance, energy, strength, and power. In business dress, red should be used only as an accent. Managers should avoid wearing red in potentially volatile situations such as evaluations, salary reviews, or terminations.

- Purple: Plum, violet, lavender, and burgundy represent creativity, inspiration, royalty, dignity, and mystery. Purple hues pair well with gray, khaki, and brown.

- Pink: A color of gentleness, sweetness, comfort, femininity, and happiness. Pink matches very well with khaki, camel, and gray. Pink is known for its soothing quality; it can soften potentially explosive situations.

- Blue: A favorite throughout the business world, blue is the color of truth, trust, security, conservatism, and masculinity.

- Green: Representing growth, tranquility, freshness, and rejuvenation, green has a calming effect. Excellent accent shades of green include moss, olive, lime, pine, and sage.

- Yellow: Represents cheer, optimism, and vitality; stimulates communication. Babies and children respond to yellow because it's the first color the eye recognizes, according to research studies. For the workplace, yellow should be muted in tone and used only as an accent.

- Orange: Linked with warmth, energy, activity, and excitement. Orange, coral, peach, and tangerine are all popular colors during the spring and summer. In muted hues, orange is the perfect color for a shirt or sweater combined with khaki pants or a khaki skirt.

- White: Traditionally associated with innocence, cleanliness, truth, and purity, white is a wonderfully sophisticated color to offset the serious tone of black, brown, gray, or navy.

37. X-FILES

Everyone's fretting these days about air travel. I'm not reluctant to fly—I just hate all those lines. To alleviate one of those lines, here's the skinny on not setting off the metal detector at x-ray checkpoints. Instead of searching yourself for the offending coin, key, watch, or other metal item, collect these things into one place beforehand. A waist-pack with a quick-release buckle, for example, can be handed easily to the attendant.

38. PHONE CARD FINESSE

One thing I hate about traveling is that hotel phone rates can resemble the national gross domestic product of Portugal. Moreover, many cell phones don't work in foreign ports of call ("No, Larry, they said they wanted 20,000 widgets—not midgets"). One tip that always works for me is to bring along a prepaid phone card from Sprint or AT&T. Any pharmacy or quickie mart carries these cards. For about $20 for two hours of phone time, prepaid phone cards usually work anyplace in the world that has a phone.

39. YOUNGER BOSS, OLDER WORKER

After you've finished reading this book and are applying some of the strategies you've learned in these pages, your firm probably will promote you right away. Uh-oh, this could mean that you'll be supervising older workers (who didn't read this book—their loss). If this happens, there may be some resentment brewing in the rank and file.

Cope with this situation by being prepared. Older workers may test you right away, so don't get defensive. In fact, expect some challenges to your leadership, and defuse them by handling each instance above board and without a hint of animosity. Troublemakers hate it when you don't take things as personally as they do.

Also, build alliances. Buttonhole some key people working for you, and bring them into your office to ask their advice. Make them feel wanted (after all, they are wanted). One last tip but a good one: Pick a situation where you can go to bat for your department and win. For example, the coffee in your department tastes like motor oil, only with much more viscosity. Lobby management for a new coffee machine or new vending machine. Your staff will love you for it— such acts demonstrate that you're all in it together.

40. KEEP TABS ON THE JOB MARKET

You don't have to be unemployed to look for employment. So don't be reluctant to test the job market to see what's out there, even if you're not looking for a job. You might even go on a job interview, just for the experience and just to see what life is like on the other side of the fence. Who knows, the grass may be greener?

41. CREATE A WEB PAGE

Go ahead, toot your own horn, especially if nobody else will. There are few better ways to do this than to build your own Web site. Throw your résumé and a cover letter on there, a picture, and a record of your accomplishments. Toss in a picture of the plaque recognizing your hole-in-one (just don't mention that it was at the local miniature golf course). When recruiters contact you, point them to it. And human resources managers at firms you want to work for will appreciate your technosavvy and the treasure trove of information you've so easily made available to them. Web sites are built easily and cheaply these days. America Online members, for example, get them for free.

42. DON'T COMPETE WITH YOUR BOSS

Everybody wants the corner office, but the last way to get there is by taking on your boss. First, you may be in the wrong and armed with poor information. Second, you'll find that no one, including your boss's boss, appreciates a worker who constantly goes over his or her supervisor's head or tries to show him or her up. If you buck your boss at every turn, downgrade his or her confidence, and generally make his or her life miserable, you'll be Swiss cheese after the bullets fly.

43. KNOW WHAT MANAGEMENT THINKS OF YOU

When all is said and done, what does your firm think of you. Loyal? Dependable? Ethical?

One way to find out is to lobby your firm or your boss to have 360-degree reviews that include colleagues, superiors, subordinates, and customers. Listen carefully to comments, and respond quickly to areas identified for improvement.

44. DOUBLE-CHECK YOUR WORK

Almost every professional has a personal horror story of overlooking a simple but critical matter, such as a missed deadline or a sensitive document accidentally e-mailed to the wrong party. Avoid such mistakes by being meticulous to the point of redundancy.

45. WANT TO GET AHEAD FASTER? WORK FOR A SMALL BUSINESS

If getting ahead for you is the key, then a small business is the place to be. You can't beat a small business for career advancement. The fast track is smaller and less crowded, and because you're apt to wear more hats in a small business, you're more attractive to other companies.

And these days, small businesses are growing faster than their bigger counterparts. Why?

- The Internet allows small companies to advertise equally with big companies.
- Small companies can profit in specialized markets—markets too small for big companies that have to sell to millions of people to be profitable.
- Small companies can change quickly if necessary. It's hard for a big companies to "turn on a dime."
- Small companies can be more innovative, particularly with respect to technology. Because a small company can change quickly, it can take advantage of new ideas faster than a big one.

46. THINK LONG TERM

Billionaire investor Warren Buffett has said that on Wall Street it's the investor with the long view who walks away with the dough.

The same is true with your career. Figure out where you want to be at age 30, age 40, age 50, and so on, and develop a blueprint to get there. Make sure to

- Constantly research your field of career interest whether you have a job or not.

- Keep an eye on trends to anticipate what will happen in your industry.

- Be open-minded. Nonstandard work is normal in today's workplace and may provide you with more opportunities than a full-time, permanent job.

- Be committed to lifelong learning. To prosper today, you will have to continuously upgrade your skills and learn new ones.

- Be an opportunity maker. Look for areas that lack skilled workers and build your knowledge in those areas.

- Be positive.

47. DON'T LISTEN TO PEOPLE WHO SAY, "IT CAN'T BE DONE"

Some people don't know jack. They're also the first ones to tell you that you're not going anywhere.

Feh! There is nothing holding you back except for your self-imposed limits. Shed them, and ignore those who don't believe in you. Realize that they don't even believe in themselves. Develop tunnel vision if you have to, but ignore the naysayers and keep moving forward. It won't be long before you leave them behind anyway.

48. REMEMBER THOMAS JEFFERSON'S "RULES FOR A GOOD LIFE"

Ten rules for the good life:

- Never put off until tomorrow what you can do today.

- Never trouble another for what you can do yourself.

- Never spend your money before you have it.

- Never buy what you do not want because it is cheap; it will never be dear to you.
- Pride costs us more than hunger, thirst, and cold.
- Never repent of having eaten too little.
- Nothing is troublesome that we do willingly.
- Don't let the evils that have never happened cost you pain.
- Always take things by their smooth handle.
- When angry, count to 10 before you speak; if very angry, count to 100.

49. READ *THE BOSS'S SURVIVAL GUIDE*

Since you are now management material, read Bob Rosner, Allan Halcrow, and Allen Levine's excellent book, *The Boss's Survival Guide* (McGraw-Hill, 2001). Everything you want to know about being the big kahuna is inside its covers.

50. DON'T FORGET RULE 50

What's rule 50? It is as follows: "Never take yourself too seriously."
What are the other rules? There are no other rules.

Index

Note: Locators in **bold** indicate assessments.

About the Author

Brian O'Connell is a former Wall Street bond trader turned freelance writer and author. His byline has appeared in dozens of national publications, including the *Wall Street Journal*, CBS News Marketwatch, and Business 2.0. He lives in Doylestown, Pennsylvania, with his wife and three children. You can reach him at briano@tradenet.net.